WELCOMING HEAVEN

J. MASSYNGBAERDE FORD

WELCOMING
HEAVEN

Prayers and Reflections for the Dying
& Those Who Love Them

XXIII
TWENTY-THIRD PUBLICATIONS
Mystic, Connecticut

Dedication

In memory of my mother
Winifred Husband Ford
whose love of literature has
inspired the form of this book.

Twenty-Third Publications
185 Willow Street
P .O. Box 180
Mystic, CT 06355
(203) 536-2611

ISBN 0-89622-442-2
Library of Congress Catalog Card Number 90-70558

Preface

"There is a divinity which shapes our ends, rough hew them though we may." The words of Shakespeare speak to us over the centuries. The desire to write this small book arose for two reasons: my own encounter with death four times and a realization that, for most Americans, death is rudely intrusive and an object of infathomable dread. I felt no fear in my brushes with our Sister Death. I deemed it a privilege when, as a nurse, I both attended the dying and prepared the deceased for their farewell services. As a New Testament scholar I have a firm belief in the resurrection of Jesus which is the everliving hope for our own re-creation.

I hope that in this book I can share my experiences, my hope, and my faith. If I can give courage and peace to one soul, it is sufficient.

Dr. J. Massyngbaerde Ford

Acknowledgments

The author and publisher of this volume acknowledge the use of quotations from these sources:

The New Book of Christian Prayers, ed. Tony Castle (New York: Crossroads Publishing Co., 1986).

(Emily Dickinson's poems) Belknap Press (of Harvard University Press) Cambridge, Massachusetts.

(Rabindranath Tagore quotes) *Death in Literature,* ed. Robert F. Weir (New York: Columbia University Press, 1980), pp. 23, 50. © Macmillan Publishing Company.

(Kahlil Gibran quote) *Death in Literature,* ed. Robert F. Weir (New York: Columbia University Press, 1980), pp. 378–379. © Alfred A. Knopf, Inc.

(Jacques Maritain quote) *Man's Destiny Is Eternity,* ed. Arthur H. Compton (Boston: Beacon Press). Appears also in *Oxford Book of Death* (New York: Oxford University Press, 1983), p. 158.

("Psalm of the Dying") *Prayers for a Planetary Pilgrim,* Edward Hays (Easton, Kansas: Forest of Peace Books, 1988), p. 187.

(Walt Whitman quote) *Death in Literature,* ed. Robert F. Weir (New York: Columbia University Press, 1980), p. 61.

(Edward Young quote) *Night Thoughts, Or the Complaint & the Consolation* (Mineola, New York: Dover Publications, 1975).

(D.H. Lawrence's "All Souls Day") *Oxford Book of Death* (New York: Oxford University Press, 1983), pp. 48–49.

(Eskimo poem) *Death in Literature,* ed. Robert F. Weir (New York: Columbia University Press, 1980, p. 368.

(C.S. Lewis quotes) *A Grief Observed* (London: Faber and Faber, 1966).

(Music) "Eye Has Not Seen" by Marty Haugen and "Jesus, Remember Me" by Jacques Bertheir. © G.I.A. Publications, Chicago, Illinois.

The author expresses her gratitude to these women for their assistance while writing this book:

Martha Turner
Sharon McMillon

CONTENTS

PART ONE—Remote Preparation

PART TWO—Proximate Preparation

PART THREE—Prayers in Mourning

A PSALM FOR THE DYING

Relatives and friends, I am about to leave;
　　my last breath does not say "goodbye,"
　　for my love for you is truly timeless,
　　beyond the touch of boney death.
I leave myself not to the undertaker,
　　for decoration in his house of the dead,
but to your memory, with love.

I leave my thoughts, my laughter, my dreams
　　to you whom I have treasured
　　beyond gold and precious gems.
I give you what no thief can steal,
　　the memories of our times together:
　　the tender, love-filled moments,
　　the successes we have shared,
　　the hard times that brought us closer together
　　and the roads we have walked side by side.

I also leave you a solemn promise
　　that after I am home in the bosom of God,
　　I will still be present,
　　whenever and wherever you call on me.
My energy will be drawn to you
　　by the magnet of our love.
Whenever you are in need, call me;
　　I will come to you,
　　with my arms full of wisdom and light
　　to open up your blocked paths,
　　to untangle your knots
　　and to be your avenue to God.

And all I take with me as I leave
　　is your love and the millions of memories
　　of all that we have shared.
So I truly enter my new life
　　as a millionaire.

Fear not nor grieve at my departure,
　　you whom I have loved so much,
　　for my roots and yours
　　are forever intertwined.
　　　　　　　　　　　　Edward Hays

PART ONE

Remote Preparation

1

Introduction

Then the Most High said,
"Call Death here to me...."
Then the unseen God said to Death,
"Come, bitter and fierce name of the world,
hide your ferocity, cover your decay,
and cast off from your self your bitterness,
and put on your youthful beauty and all your glory,
and go down to my friend Abraham
and take him and conduct him to me.
But I also tell you now that you may not terrify him;
but rather you are to take him with soft speech,
because he is my true friend."

(Testament of Abraham)

The Two Faces of Death

A short Jewish work dated about 100 years after Christ, the *Testament of Abraham* is a legend about the approaching death of Abraham, the patriarch of the Jewish people. God loved Abraham and sought to break the news of death gently to him. First, God sent the archangel Michael to warn Abraham about his approaching death. Then God commanded Death himself to go to Abraham. The patriarch was shown the pleasing aspect of Death, but he also asked to see the horrendous side. Both presentations had a profound effect upon him. Because of Abraham's faithful and service-oriented life, however, God told Death to clothe himself again in all his glory. Thus Abraham departed with joy and peace to the heavenly academy.

The *Testament of Abraham* shows various features that we ourselves connect with death, particularly the two different aspects of death, and our natural reluctance to leave the known world and go to one unknown, however much promised joy there is ahead.

Death's Image in the Contemporary World

The *Testament of Abraham* has a peculiar relevance for us today. We, too, are surrounded by Death in its most horrendous form, the "abominable countenance and merciless look" described by the *Testament*. We see death through war, through urban violence, through famine, through earthquake, flood, fire, and hurricane, and most of all, through the torture rampant in so many countries. We also see death consuming people through many kinds of illness, including, most dramatically, AIDS.

Although death is all around us, our culture has somehow made death seem less natural. We see less of death in our homes because the sick are in hospitals or hospices. So often we do not even experience the short life span of animals. We do not rejoice through their birth nor grieve with their death. We live in a society that nonchalantly throws away anything that is worn or disliked or not immediately useful. Many have no qualms about violently and painfully killing a defenseless baby in the womb.

We live in a materialistic, comfortable culture that dwells on death, but seems willing to go to almost any length to deny its reality. Movies and television shows cultivate a macabre and bloody prospect of death, especially for children, but they also give us the illusion that death is not final; dead heroes and heroines reappear in subsequent episodes. Reports of space research and organ transplants also encourage us to hope for immortality in this life and, in the process, help to weaken our unique Christian view of the afterlife. By prolonging our life expectancy, advanced technology can heighten our human hope for the splendor of this life, but it can also help to trap us by giving us "existence" rather than "life."

Restoring the Balance

We need to do more as individuals, as families, and as communities to counter the death-denying aspects of our culture and to prepare for death and the afterlife. We, like God and Abraham, must seek to make a friend of Death and to live our lives with calm fortitude and peaceful expectation of a future full of felicity. We need to cultivate a healthier attitude toward what St. Francis of Assisi called "Our Sister Death," and such cultivation takes time, patience, effort, and gentleness. We need to see Death in its youthful beauty and glory. This we can do because Christ has won the victory over Death (1 Corinthians 25:54–58).

We need to see death not so much as an end, and a gruesome one at that, but as the threshold of new life, a rite of passage. Death is like a second birth. Like the first birth, it has a gestation period and is attended with labor and pain. When a child is born, the mother and father tend to forget the pain and think only of the joy. Jesus in John's Gospel speaks of this (John 16:21). In *Other-Worldly Journeys* (New York: Oxford University Press, 1987), Carol Zaleski reports the words of one "near-death experience" person:

> It's just as though you're being held in a cradle of love, and just being carried to the most beautiful magical story God could ever create.

It may be very difficult for young persons to think of their own death, but as we grow older, making a remote preparation for death is both natural and wise. The words of Teilhard de Chardin are fitting:

> When the signs of age begin to mark my body and still more when they touch my mind; when the illness that is to diminish me or carry me off strikes from without or is born

within me; when the painful moment comes in which I suddenly awaken to the fact that I am ill or growing old; in all
those dark moments, O God, grant that I may understand
that it is you, provided only my faith is strong enough, who
are painfully parting the fibres of my being in order to pen-
etrate to the very marrow of my substance and bear me
away within yourself.

Remote Preparation for Death

There are many ways to begin making a remote preparation
for death and the afterlife. Here are some thoughts about the
most important of them.

Development of the Idea of Heaven   Except in the Apocalypse,
scriptural passages about heaven are difficult to find. When we
read the Scriptures prayerfully, however, we can highlight passages that deal with death, the next life, and the presence of the
divine. Examples include Jacob's dream (Genesis 28:10–22);
God's revelation through a "still small voice" to Elijah on Horeb
(1 Kings 19:9–13); the Transfiguration of Jesus (Luke 9:28–36); 2
Corinthians 12:1–10 where Paul speaks about the power of God
tabernacling over him in his weakest moments (verse 10); and
passages about the resurrection, particularly 2 Maccabees 7; Dan-
iel 12:1–3; 1 Corinthians 2:6–16 ("Eye hath not seen...."). We can
then use these passages with those to whom we minister, and we
can also turn to some non-biblical literature, such as the works of
Shakespeare, as I have done in this book.

Other-Worldly Journeys   Throughout Christian literature, there
is a tradition of "other-worldly journeys." Some are mere flights
of fancy; all are culturally conditioned, but some bear a sharp
sense of reality, a reality borne out by the changed, sincere lives
of those who have undergone near-death experiences. Modern
research has added to our findings, although one must interpret
this research with great care.

We might with profit—and I speak tentatively here—

examine some of the near-death experiences from reliable sources, for they appear to mitigate the fear of dying and death. Interesting, for example, is the kind of interrogation undergone by the "near-death experience" person. It is not frightening or condemnatory but:

> The being, all seem to agree, does not direct the question to them to accuse or threaten them for they still feel the total love and acceptance coming from the light, no matter what their answer may be. Rather, the point of the question seems to be to make them think about their lives, to draw them out.
> (Carol Zaleski, *Other Worldly Experiences*)

We may compare this to Matthew 25:31–40 where the Son of Humanity comes not to condemn but to reveal the unconscious acts of loving kindness that good people have done.

Experiencing the Presence of God   Third, we must attempt to sense the presence of God in our daily life. This is done chiefly, but not exclusively, in prayer. One example of a sense of the presence of God is the following:

> This person is accustomed to practice the experience of the presence of God in three ways. The first is by the way of the memory....The second is by the way of understanding; the soul knows without any reasoning...how God is in her. By this knowledge she comes to feel the presence of God within her, God giving her the grace of communicating Himself to her in this manner. This feeling of the presence of God is not obtained by way of the imagination; but it is in her as a certitude received from on high; she has a spiritual and experiential certitude, that God is in the soul and in all places. This presence of God is called an intellectual presence....
> (A. Poulain, "Life of Alphonsus" in *Graces of Interior Prayer*. London: Routledge and Kegan Paul Ltd., 1957)

The experience of God is, of course, not restricted to prayer.

We can also feel the presence of God by pouring as much beauty, peace, and vitality as we can into our souls. Music, song, dance, classical literature, nature, scientific endeavors and the joy of discovery in general, the love of other human beings, the birth of a baby, gardening, thinking back on ennobling experiences and achievements of any kind can all help us cultivate beauty and reach out to a loving God. In this way, the most treasured moments of our life will become an anticipation of eternal life itself.

Belief in the Resurrection　The Christian who accepts the central doctrine of Christianity, namely, that through Jesus all humanity can expect an eternal, transformed life similar to Christ's after the resurrection, should not find it difficult to meditate on the afterlife. It is important to realize, however, that a belief in resurrection is not belief in resuscitation. Resurrection is part of the whole and complete cosmic renewal of which Paul speaks in Romans 8:18–30. Our life will be transformed and changed, but personhood will still remain. Although we do not know precisely what God has in store for us, we must nurture a firm belief in the afterlife as the consummation and climax to which all lives are aspiring. We also should not hesitate to pray to our loved ones who have departed or to the modern-day martyrs and confessors in so many countries of the world.

Night and Morning Prayer　Night and Morning Prayer can kindle our hope of new life. The night draws a veil and a limit to wrongdoing, and gives quiet growth toward good. Waking from sleep in the morning is a potent reminder of the new life ahead. Sleep is sometimes called the shadow of death. Waking should remind us of the resurrection of Jesus and our resurrection that will bring a new beginning and a new creation. At night we can add a prayer for a happy death, and for new faith and an understanding of heaven. Listen to an ancient prayer found in the Gelasian sacramentary:

> God, through the mighty resurrection of your Son Jesus Christ
>   you have liberated us from the power of darkness
> and brought us into the kingdom of your love;

      grant that as he was raised from the dead
by the glory of the Father,
      so may we walk in newness of life,
and look for those things which are in heaven,
      where with you, Father and the Holy Spirit,
he is alive and reigns for ever and ever. Amen.

The Sacraments For Catholics and other members of the liturgical churches, it is good to remember that all the sacraments, especially the eucharist, bring us into union with the resurrected Christ and thereby link heaven and earth. The sacraments of reconciliation and anointing of the sick also provide rites of passage that enable us to approach death and the afterlife in strength, peace, and hope. Roman Catholics recall that the *Ave Maria* (Hail Mary) contains a prayer for a happy death. We also have the example of innumerable saints before us who can help us see that we live in the promise of ineffable hope and surprise.

The Celebration of Sunday Finally, one of the best ways of remote preparation for death and the afterlife is by restoring a sense of Sunday celebration and by recovering the spiritual meaning of this day. In contrast to the fever and clamor of much of modern Western culture—and increasingly in the so-called Third World—Sunday can speak of the love of silence and peace lauded by many of the ancient writers and by many contemplative people today.

The Sabbath (or Sunday) can be a time when we shake off the tyranny of modern technology, especially the telephone and the computer. It is the time, says Abraham Heschel, when we do not seek to acquire, but rather we "are"; we seek not to control but to share, not to be dominating but to be in harmony.

The theology of the Sabbath is extremely rich and encompasses the themes of creation, redemption, and final restoration. It knits together the present, the past, and the future as well as human nature and God. It is the root of cosmic faith. The Sabbath celebrates both the beginning of the world and the beginning of humanity. Philo, a Hellenistic Jew living about the time of Christ, said that

We are told that this world was made in six days and that on the seventh God ceased from his works and began to contemplate what had been so well created, and therefore he bade those who should live as citizens under this world-order to follow God in this as in other matters.

For the Jewish people, the Sabbath is more than a day of rest. It is also a memorial of redemption, a day commemorating their escape from slavery in Egypt. When the children of Israel entered into Canaan, they entered into the land of rest. On the Sabbath, therefore, God is celebrated as liberator. But the Sabbath also looks toward the days of the Messiah when all the nations will be gathered and all will be redeemed. Philo says:

> The festival is not of a single city or country but of the universe, and it alone strictly deserves to be called public, as belonging to all people.

The Sabbath is an anticipation of this world to come. It is the day on which God offers peace and fellowship to all creatures. It celebrates creation, liberation, covenant-consecration, redemption, and eschatological restoration.

Jesus himself kept the Sabbath, but he also chose to perform acts of healing on this day. Although at times Jesus appears to break the regulations with regard to the Sabbath, he is actually restoring its redemptive, healing, and joyful qualities. He placed both a new emphasis and a new theology on the Sabbath and used it as a day on which he could help the poor and needy. Jesus acted as Creator-Liberator-Healer. On the Sabbath, God raises the dead, gives life, and conducts saving judgment; Jesus and his followers do the same. God raised Jesus from the dead on the day after the Sabbath, and this day, the first day of the work week, became the Christian Sunday, a day of rest, peace, and rejoicing.

Early Christian writers often referred to Sunday as the eighth day, not only because it began a new week, but because it was the day of the Lord's resurrection and often the day of baptism. Through baptism on this day, we die with Christ, and are cleansed from sin so that we might be given the Spirit and a share in Christ's risen life. Just as the Jewish infant boy was circumcised on the eighth day, so the whole soul of the Christian is born of God and purified in baptism. The eighth day was thus the beginning of a new way of life, a new creation. It symbolized the new and eternal world being transformed by God in Christ. It symbolized the world of the Spirit, the world of the risen One who appeared to his disciples on Sunday, the "first day of the week," who passed the Spirit onto them in a breath, and who said to them, "Peace be with you" (John 20:19–22). The dying and rising, and victory and peace of Christ is thus at the very center of the Christian Sunday. Augustine of Hippo, in his "Commentary on Psalm 91:2" states:

> One whose conscience is good, tranquil . . . this peace is the Sabbath of the heart. For, indeed, it is directed toward the hope of Him Who promises, and although one suffers at the present time, he looks forward toward the hope of Him Who is to come, and then all the clouds of sorrow will be dispersed. This present joy, in the peace of our hope, is our Sabbath.

In another work, Augustine also prays:

> O, Lord God, Thou who hast given us all, grant us Thy peace, the peace of rest, the peace of the Sabbath, the peace without an evening.

2

Services for Sunday

I

For that which draws near to God enters into affinity with what it is, and through that immutability becomes self-standing. And when the mind is at rest it recognizes clearly how great a blessing rest is and, struck with wonder at its beauty, has the thought that it belongs either to God alone or to that form of being which is midway between mortal and immortal kind. Thus he says: "And I stood between the Lord and you" (Deuteronomy 5:5), where he does not mean that he stood firm upon his feet, but wishes to indicate that the mind of the Sage, released from storms and wars, with calm still weather and profound peace around it, is superior to human beings, but less than God.

(Philo, *On Dreams*)

Suggested Scripture: John 20:19–23

Prayer
O God our Creator, you rested on the seventh day
    and contemplated the beauty and harmony of your universe.
Help us to pause and reflect
    upon the gifts and the friends that you have given us,
    and grant us that lively hope which looks beyond death
    to the new creation.
    Amen.

Grant, Lord, that we may live in your fear,
die in your favour,
rest in your peace,
rise in your power
and reign in your glory;
for your own beloved Son's sake,
Jesus Christ our Lord.
   (William Laud)

V. May God grant us the grace of contemplation
R. And the wisdom to discern good from evil.
V. May God grace our souls with peace
R. And our hearts with compassion.

Dismissal

May God send us forth this week with high hopes,
ever-mindful of our eternal destiny. Amen.

II

. . . (the Sabbath is) a period of timelessness set off from
the week, when our moving frantic activities come to
a slow halt and a sense of unutterable peace, soul-calm,
and a tranquility can begin to be felt.
   (*The Jewish Catalogue*)

Suggested Scripture: John 14:27–28

Prayer

God of peace and rest,
 bless us with your creative peace
  that our souls, minds, and bodies may be refreshed on this day.
Let it be a foreshadowing of the life to come
 when the "busy beat" of time will cease
 and your friends will come to live in joyful harmony.
Amen.

Abide with us, Lord, for it is toward evening
and the day is far spent;
abide with us and with your whole church.
Abide with us in the evening of the day,
in the evening of life,
in the evening of the world.
Abide with us and with all your faithful ones, O Lord,
in time and eternity.

(Lutheran Manual of Prayer)

V. May God grant us the grace to modify our activity
R. And to move harmoniously through our lives.
V. May God grant relief to those in pain
R. And peace to those of troubled mind.

Dismissal
May the grace of Jesus be with us,
that in our activity
we do not lose the sight of eternity. Amen.

III

The Logos has transferred by the new alliance the celebration of the Sabbath to the rising of the light. He has given us a type of the true rest in the saving day of the Lord, the first day of the sun, when we gather after the interval of six days, we celebrate the holy and spiritual Sabbaths....All things whatsoever that were prescribed for the Sabbath, we have transferred them to the Lord's Day, as being more authoritative and more highly regarded and first in rank, and more honorable than the Jewish Sabbath. In fact, it is on this day of the creation of the world that God said: "Let there be light and there was light." It is also on this day that the Sun of Justice has risen in our souls.

(Eusebius, *Commentary on Psalm 91*)

Suggested Scripture: John 20:11–18

Prayer
Jesus, you taught us the true meaning of the day of rest.
You made it a day of healing and joy.
Grant rest to your war-torn world,
    the light of justice to those who oppress others,
    relief to the suffering,
    and the joy of salvation to your people.
On this day, teach us to practice peace, care, and harmony
    in anticipation of the world to come.
    Amen.

O Lord, evening is at hand, furnish it with brightness.
As day has its evening so also has life;
the even of life is age, age has overtaken me,
furnish it with brightness.
Cast me not away in the time of age;
forsake me not when my strength faileth me.
Do Thou make, do Thou bear, do Thou carry and deliver me.
Abide with me, Lord, for it is toward evening,
and the day is far spent of this fretful life.
Let Thy strength be made perfect in my weakness.

(Lancelot Andrews)

V. May God grant rest to the weary
R. And compassion to the oppressors.
V. May God heal the sick
R. And give food to the hungry.

Dismissal
    May the Holy Spirit dwell with us
    so that we may be life-bearing vessels of God's hope. Amen.

IV

Behold the day of the Lord to be venerable and solemn,
because on it the Savior, like the rising sun, conquered

the darkness of the underworld and gleamed in the glory
of the resurrection. This is why the same day was called
the Day of the Sun by the pagans, because the Sun of
Justice once risen dies no more.

(Maximus of Turin)

Suggested Scripture: Psalm 8

Prayer
God of grace,
  grant that this day of peace
  may quiet our frantic lives and our dread of death.
May each sunrise make us mindful of the resurrection of your Son
  and of all those who follow in his footsteps.
  Amen.

  Lord, who said that at midnight,
  at an hour we least expect,
  the Bridegroom shall come;
  grant that the cry, "the Bridegroom cometh,"
  may sound continually in all ears
  so that we may never be unprepared
  to go out and meet our Lord and Savior, Jesus Christ.

(Lancelot Andrews)

V. May God grant faith to those in despair
R. And comfort to those who mourn.
V. May God retrieve those who are missing or been made
  hostage
R. And cheer the imprisoned in mind and body.

Dismissal
  May we carry the light of Christ
  to kindle hope within the world. Amen.

V

May Christ-Omega keep me always young "to the greater
glory of God." For

old age comes from him
old age leads on to him, and
old age will touch me only in so far as he wills.
To be "young" means to be hopeful, energetic, smiling—
and clear-sighted.

May I accept death in whatever guise it may come to
me in Christ-Omega, that is within the process of the
development of life.

A smile (inward and outward) means facing with sweetness
and gentleness whatever befalls me.

Jesus-Omega, grant me to serve you, to proclaim you,
to glorify you, to make you manifest, to be the very end
through all the time that remains to me of life, and above
all through my death. Desperately, Lord Jesus, I commit
to your care my last active years, and my death; do not
let them impair or spoil my work I have so dreamed of
achieving for you.
(Pierre Teilhard de Chardin)

Suggested Scripture: 2 Corinthians 5:1–9

Prayer
God of time and eternity,
we commit into your gentle hands the manner of our death.
Grant that we may have clarity of mind,
freedom in spirit, peace of soul,
and, if it seems good, ease of body.
May our loved ones surround us and may our hope be in you.
Amen.

Lord, support us all the day long,
until the shadows lengthen and the evening comes,
and the busy world is hushed,
and the fever of life is over,
and our work is done.
Then, Lord, in thy mercy,
grant us a safe lodging, and a holy rest, and peace at the last;
through Jesus Christ our Lord.
(John Henry Newman)

V. May God be present to those who face death
R. And inspire them with the hope of everlasting life.
V. May God make the declining years of men and women years
 of grace and service
R. And may they share their wisdom with the young.

Dismissal
 May the eternity of God give meaning to our lives
 so that we may live with cheerful hearts. Amen.

VI

O God
 my God
 keep me from flinching/waning
 slumbering into that timeless rest
 that never is
keep me from falling into a prison
 of egotistical habits
 where the bars
 are superficial friends
 and drinks
 and stupid laughter
 kisses without love
 business and organization
 without heart
 and gifts for self-flattery
 these bars that prevent life evolving
 towards that taste of the infinite
 open to your call...
 break down those barriers
 that prevent me living, my God.
 (Jean Vanier)

Suggested Scripture: Philippians 4:8–9

Prayer

God, our Father and our Mother,
    you created everything with artistry and design.
Keep us from marring your creative talent.
Teach us to hold all life in delicate trust,
    with serious but joyous care.
Help us not to be wanton with your gifts,
    and bestow on us the charism of discernment
    to see the true values of all human beings
    and of the universe.
Amen.

Lead me from death
To life, from falsehood to truth.

Lead me from despair
To hope, from fear to trust.
Lead me from hate
To love, from war to peace.

Let peace fill our heart,
Our world, our universe.
                    (International Prayer for Peace)

V. May God teach us the wisdom of living
R. And make our lives a source of joy to others.
V. May God forgive our wasted hours
R. And allow our future to brighten the lives of others.

Dismissal

    May I be no person's enemy,
    and may I be the friend of that which is eternal and abides.
                                        (Eusebius)

VII

Behold, how good and pleasant it is

when brothers and sisters dwell in unity!
It is like the precious oil upon the head,
   running down upon the beard,
   upon the beard of Aaron,
   running down on the collar of his robes!
It is like the dew of Hermon,
   which falls on the mountains of Zion!
For there the Lord has commanded the blessing,
   life for evermore.

(Psalm 33)

Rejoice in the Lord always; again I will say, Rejoice.
   Let all people know your forbearance.
   The Lord is at hand.
Have no anxiety about anything,
   but in everything by prayer and supplication with thanksgiving
   let your requests be made known to God.
And the peace of God,
   which passes all understanding,
   will keep your hearts and your minds
   in Christ Jesus.
Finally, brothers and sisters,
   whatever is true,
   whatever is honorable,
   whatever is just,
   whatever is pure,
   whatever is lovely,
   whatever is gracious,
   if there is any excellence,
   if there is anything worthy of praise,
   think about these things.

What you have heard and received
   and heard and seen in me,
   do;
   and the God of peace will be with you.

(Philippians 4:4–9)

Prayer

God of death and life, grant us tranquility of mind and gratitude
for your blessings even though we may be in pain.

Give us a hungry desire for all that is gracious, beautiful, and life
giving

and prepare us for that life where all conflict, pain, and brutality
melt before the gracious smile of our Savior, Jesus Christ.

Prayer

Grant unto us, O Lord, the royalty of inward happiness
and the serenity which comes from living close to
thee. Daily renew in us the sense of joy, and let thy
eternal spirit dwell in our souls and bodies, filling
every corner of our hearts with light and gladness: so
that, bearing about with us the infection of a good
courage, we may be diffusers of life, and meet all that
comes, of good or ill, even death itself, with gallant
and high-hearted happiness: giving thee thanks always
for all things.

(Robert Louis Stevenson)

O Lord, I rejoice and am exceeding glad;
Because of thy goodness,
In creating the world.
But much more abundantly,
For the glory of my soul;
Which cut out of nothing thou hast builded
To be a temple unto God,
A living temple of thine omnipresence,
An understanding eye,
A temple of eternity,
A temple of wisdom, blessedness, and glory.
O ye powers of mine immortal Soul, bless ye the Lord,
praise him and magnify him for ever.
He hath made you greater,
More glorious, brighter,
Better than the heavens.
The heaven of heavens,

A meeter dwelling place for his eternal Godhead
Than the heaven of heavens.
The heaven of heavens,
And all the spaces above the heavens,
Are not able to contain him.
Being but dead and silent places,
They feel not themselves.
They know nothing,
See no immensity or wideness at all.
But in thee, my soul, there is a perceptive power
To measure all spaces beyond the heavens
And those spaces
By him into thee
To feel and see the heaven of heavens
All things contained in them,
And his presence in thee.
Nor canst thou only feel his omnipresence in thee,
But adore his goodness,
Dread his power,
Reverence his majesty,
See his wisdom,
Rejoice in his bounty,
Conceive his eternity,
Praise his glory.
Which being things transcendent unto place,
Cannot by the heavens at all be apprehended.
With reverence, O God, and dread mixed with joy,
I come before thee.
To consider thy glory in the perfection of my soul
The workmanship of the Lord.

(Thomas Traherne)

V. May we see beyond our physical lives
R. And rejoice in the creativity of our minds and souls;
V. May God grant us common sense
R. And a perennial gift of good humor.

Dismissal

The Lord bless you and keep you:
The Lord make his (her) face to shine upon you,
    and be gracious to you:
The Lord lift up his (her) countenance upon you,
    and give you peace.
"So shall they put my name upon the people of Israel,
    and I will bless them."

(Numbers 6:24–27)

3

Morning Prayers

I

SHEMA (recited as sunrise and sunset)

Hear, O Israel:
The Lord our God is one Lord;
    and you shall love the Lord your God with all your heart,
    and with all your soul,
    and with all your might.

And these words which I command you this day shall be upon
your heart;
    and you shall teach them diligently to your children,
    and shall talk of them when you sit in your house,
    and when you walk by the way,
    and when you lie down,
    and when you rise.

And you shall bind them as a sign upon your hand,
    and they shall be as frontlets between your eyes.
    And you shall write them on the doorposts of your house
    and on your gates.
                       (Deuteronomy 6:4–9)

Scripture Reading: Hosea 6:3

Let us know, let us press on to know the Lord;

the Lord's going forth is sure as the dawn;
the Lord will come to us as the showers,
   as the spring rains that water the earth.
                    (Hosea 6:3)

Prayer
God, our Creator, your timeless, unerring love
   is renewed for us with each dawn.
Fill our souls with the melody and harmony of your
   universe and a lively expectation of meeting you,
our Creator, face to face. Amen.

V. May God grant to the dying a glimpse of God's glory
R. And make their journey through death peaceful.
V. May God bless all caretakers and companions of the dying
R. That they may know what joy they bring to God.

Dismissal
May the certainty of Christ's coming reign in our hearts. Amen.

II

Bless the Lord, O my soul!
   O Lord my God, thou art very great!
Thou art clothed with honor and majesty,
   who coverest thyself with light as with a garment,
who has stretched out the heavens like a tent,
   who hast laid the beams of thy chambers on the waters,
   who ridest on the wings of the wind,
who makest the winds thy messengers,
      fire and flame thy ministers.
                    (Psalm 104)

Prayer
O God, artist beyond compare, you have fashioned your world
   and ours to be a source of constant wonder and beauty
   for its inhabitants.

Grant us this day to be alert and receptive to your presence
   and plant within us the excitement of coming into your
   presence for eternity. Amen.

V. May the inhabitants of the earth respect her and show kindness to her;
R. May God teach us to be true and just stewards of the gifts of
   creation.
V. May God bless those to whom he (she) has given the talent of
   music, poetry or art,
R. That we may adorn the world with beauty.

Dismissal
May the artistry of God touch our hearts. Amen.

III

She [Wisdom] will come to meet him like a mother,
   and like the wife of his youth she will welcome him.
She will feed him with the bread of understanding,
   and give him the water of wisdom to drink.
He will lean on her and will not fall, and he will
   rely on her and will not be put to shame.
   . . .
He will find gladness and a crown of rejoicing,
   and will acquire an everlasting name.
                          (Sirach 15:2–4, 6)

Prayer
God of all Wisdom, our days are often spent in procuring
   what seems to us the essential needs, especially for the body.
Grant us to thirst after true wisdom and the peerless cup of
   understanding to find undying joy. Amen.

V. May the Holy Spirit be like a Mother to us.
R. May she give special care to orphans.

V. May she share her maternity with parents
R. And nurture children in her wisdom.

Dismissal
May the joy of the Spirit warm our hearts and grace our speech.
Amen.

IV

Scripture Reading: John 6:46–51

Prayer
Loving God, we awake to the joy and discovery of a new day.
Grant that we may gain in wisdom and experience and look
   forward to
   that life which brings everything to completion. Amen.

V. May God grant that we do not sleep through life
R. Or be heedless of the needs of others.
V. May God bring us to intimacy with Jesus
R. And to share his grace with others.

Dismissal
May the hope of eternity strengthen us in all our trials. Amen.

V

Let not your hearts be troubled; believe in God,
   believe also in me.
In my Father's house are many rooms; if it were not so,
   would I have told you that I go to prepare a place for you?
And when I go and prepare a place for you, I will come again
   and will take you to myself, that where I am you may be also.
                                                    (John 14:1–3)

Prayer
Gracious Spirit, in your maternal love,
inspire us to be good homemakers.
May the love that we share with one another
be an earnest of that time
when we shall be wholly wrapped in your divine love.
Amen.

V. May God inspire us with quiet confidence
R. And gentleness (graciousness) of manner.
V. May God give us the grace of nurturing
R. And make us prodigal with her (his) love.

Dismissal
May the peace of Christ reign in our hearts and minds.

VI

I am the resurrection and the life:
whoever believes in me,
though he (she) should die, will come to life;
and whoever is alive and believes in me
will never die.

(John 11:25–26)

Prayer
Jesus, first born of the dead, let each new morning awake within
us the desire and hope for the resurrected life.
Teach us to reverence our own bodies and those of others as
temples of the Holy Spirit. Heal our blindness and enable us
to see in each person a glimpse of your deity. Amen.

V. May God grant us faith in the resurrection
R. And a reverence for our bodies.
V. May God give us understanding of life
R. And a desire to promote all that is good.

Dismissal
May we carry a staunch faith in Christ in our souls. Amen.

VII

When Israel was a child, I loved him,
    and out of Egypt I called my son…
Yet it was I who taught Ephraim to walk,
    I took them up in my arms;
    but they did not know that I healed them.
I led them with cords of compassion,
    with the bands of love,
and I became to them as one who eases the yoke on their jaws,
    and I bend down to them and fed them.

(Hosea 11:1, 3–4)

Prayer
God, teach us to become nurturers of one another,
    of the earth, and of ourselves.
Give us the patience to cultivate all the potential
    you have planted within us.
    You plant, we water, and
    you give the increase. Amen.

V. May God teach us to draw the disturbed with the bonds of
    love.
R. May God grant us the grace to walk as healers.
V. May God help us to forgive ourselves and others
R. And to experience God's own redeeming love.

Dismissal
May God walk with us to teach us to create, not destroy. Amen.

4

Night Prayers

When the perishable puts on the imperishable, and the mortal puts on immortality, then shall come to pass the saying that is written: "Death is swallowed up in victory. O death, where is thy victory? O death, where is thy sting?" The sting of death is sin, and the power of sin is the law. But thanks be to God, who gives us the victory through our Lord Jesus Christ. Therefore, my beloved brothers and sisters, be steadfast, immovable, always abounding in the work of the Lord, knowing that in the Lord your labor is not in vain.

(1 Corinthians 15:54–58)

Prayer
God, you provide the day for labor
  and the night for rest.
In the healing of sleep let us sense the
  future healing of the human person when we will
  rise gloriously to our full potential. Amen.

V. May God grant us fruitful work
R. And a sense of responsibility towards others.
V. May God grant us the belief of victory over death
R. And hope for immortality.

Dismissal
May the resurrected Christ accompany us in all our ways. Amen.

II

But the righteous one, though he (she) die early, will be at rest.
For old age is not honored for length of time,
   nor measured by number of years;
but understanding is gray hair for men and women,
   and a blameless life is ripe old age.
There was one who pleased God and was loved by God,
   and while living among sinners he (she) was taken up.
. . .
Being perfected in a short time, he (she) fulfilled long years...
(Wisdom 4:7–10, 13)

Prayer
O God, arising from sleep and re-entering the world,
   we think of those who have slept the sleep of death
   and been transported into everlasting life.
Help us to feel their succoring presence,
   to forgive their follies of the past,
   and to treasure the memory of their goodness.
   Amen.

V. May God grant us quality rather than quantity of life
R. And succor those who find no meaning in life.
V. May God comfort those who lost their loved ones at an early
   age
R. And grant that their memory may be a treasure to many.

Dismissal
May God keep us mindful of the "swift celerity" of life and make
each day meaningful. Amen.

III

But the souls of the righteous are in the hand of God,
   and no torment will ever touch them.

In the eyes of the foolish they seemed to have died,
   and their departure was thought to be an affliction,
and their going from us to be their destruction;
   but they are at peace.
For though in the sight of men and women they were punished,
   their hope is full of immortality.
Having been disciplined a little, they will receive great good,
   because God tested them and found them worthy;
like gold in the furnace God tried them, and like a sacrificial
   burnt offering God accepted them.
In the time of their visitation they will shine forth, and will
   run like sparks through the stubble.

They will govern nations and rule over peoples, and the
   Lord will reign over them for ever.
                              (Wisdom 3:1–8)

Prayer
O God, you have brought us to the close of another day
   and to the opportunity for rest and peace.
May this rest be an anticipation of that life
   which knows no sunset
   but clothes us in the timelessness
   and gladness of eternity. Amen.

V. May God grant that we be full of the hope of immortality
R. And make our hope contagious.
V. May God comfort the lonely
R. And tabernacle over those crushed in spirit.

Dismissal
May God make us a tonic to the oppressed in mind and body.
Amen.

IV

Then I saw a new heaven and a new earth; for the first

heaven and the first earth had passed away, and the sea was no more. And I saw the holy city, new Jerusalem, coming down out of heaven from God, prepared as a bride adorned for her husband, and I heard a great voice from the throne saying, "Behold, the dwelling of God is with the human race. He will dwell with them, and they shall be God's people, and God will be with them; God will wipe away every tear from their eyes, and death shall be no more, neither shall there be mourning nor crying nor pain any more, for the former things have passed away."

(Revelation 21:1–4)

Prayer

O God, you draw the veil of night over the joys and mistakes of our day
    so that each day give us a new beginning and new opportunities.
Lift our minds to that night
    which will be the prelude to our eternal day. Amen

V. May God give us a sense of the newness of life
R. And its unfolding wonders and opportunities.
V. May God speak tenderly to the afflicted
R. And give special wisdom to the unlettered and those overwhelmed by life.

Dismissal

May God make us a source of inspiration and a receptacle of good will. Amen

V

The wolf shall dwell with the lamb,
and the leopard shall lie down with the kid,
and the calf and the lion and the fatling together,
and a little child shall lead them.
The cow and the bear shall feed;

their young shall lie down together;
and the lion shall eat straw like the ox.
The sucking child shall play over the hole of the asp,
and the weaned child shall put his hand on the adder's den.
They shall not hurt or destroy in all my holy mountain;
for the earth shall be full of the knowledge of the Lord
as the waters cover the sea.

(Isaiah 11:6–9)

Prayer
O Creator God, each night with rhythmic care
    you cause the maternal sea to wash clean
    the sands of human carelessness and children's play.
So let the mighty ocean of your love
    wash away our mistakes and sins
    so that we begin to experience that time
    when the sea will be no more
    and human potential be unfettered and unerring.
    Amen.

V. May God grant us to cultivate a sensitivity to Mother Earth
R. And bring man, woman, and animals to mutual understanding.
V. May God bless scientists with wisdom
R. And a genuine sense of the preciousness of nature.

Dismissal
May God grant that we may walk in harmony with nature and with human beings. Amen.

VI

Come to me, all who labor and are heavy laden, and I will give you rest. Take my yoke upon you, and learn from me; for I am gentle and lowly in heart, and you will find rest for your souls. For my yoke is easy, and my burden is light.

(Matthew 11:28–30)

Prayer
Jesus, you knew the fatigue and frustration of labor,
   to you we commend our weary bodies and troubled minds.
Send to us refreshings from your Spirit
   and let the dove of peace rest over our dwellings
   until that time when every pain and tear shall be obliterated.
Amen.

V. May God teach us to be persons of rest
R. And instruments of peace.
V. May God enlighten the burdens of the oppressed
R. And give peace to the souls of the departed.

Dismissal
May the Holy Spirit teach us to bring rest to the weary.

VII

Then he called for Solomon his son, and charged him to build a house for the Lord, the God of Israel. David said to Solomon, My son, I had it in my heart to build a house to the name of the Lord my God. But the word of the Lord came to me, saying "You have shed much blood and have waged great war; you shall not build a house to my name, because you have shed so much blood before me upon the earth. Behold, a son shall be born to you; he shall be a man of peace. I will give him peace from all his enemies round about; for his name shall be Solomon, and I will give peace and quiet to Israel in his days."

(1 Chronicles 22:6–9)

Prayer
God of peace, teach us to be men and women of rest.
   As we begin to take our nightly repose we beseech you
   to send your mercy on all those who have no domestic peace

and all those in war-torn countries.
Let our world build houses of security and joy
for all its inhabitants. Amen.

V. May God bring peace upon the war-wrought earth
R. And rest to disquieted souls.
V. May God deliver the bonds of those fettered
   by drink or by drugs or lethal powers
R. And fill us all with the vigor of the divine Spirit.

Dismissal
May God make us heralds of peace and reapers of justice.

Reflections
    God, I am travelling out to death's sea,
    I, who exulted in sunshine and laughter,
    Thought not of dying—death is such waste of me!—
    Grant me one prayer: Doom not the hereafter
    of mankind to war, as though I had died not—
    I, who in battle, my comrade's arm linking,
    Shouted and sang—life in my pulses hot
    Throbbing and dancing! Let not my sinking
    In dark be for naught my death a vain thing!
    God, let me know it the end of man's fever!
    Make my last breath a bugle call, carrying
    Peace o'er the valleys and cold hills for ever!
                                    (John Galsworthy)

    "Remember me" implored the Thief—
    Oh Magnanimity!
    My Visitor in Paradise
    I give thee Guaranty.
    That Courtesy will fair remain
    When the Delight is Dust
    With which we cite this Mightiest case
    Of Compensated Trust.

Of All, we are allowed to hope
But Affidavit stands
That this was due, where some, we fear
Are unexpected friends
                    (Emily Dickinson)

If my Bark sink
'Tis to another sea-
Mortality's Ground Floor
Is Immortality
                    (Emily Dickinson)

That sacred Closet when you sweep-
Entitled "Memory"—
Select a reverential Broom—
And do it silently.
                    (Emily Dickinson)

PART TWO

Proximate Preparation

5

On Entering the Hospital

At the door of a Christian hospital:

O God,
  make the door of this house wide enough
  to receive all who need human love and fellowship,
  and a heavenly Father's care;
  and narrow enough to shut out
  all envy, pride, and hate.
Make its threshold smooth enough
  to be no stumbling-block to children,
  nor to straying feet,
  but rugged enough to turn back the tempter's power:
  make it a gateway to thine eternal life.
                              (Bishop Thomas Ken)

When you enter a hospital you open yourself to the sacred art of healing. Healing is sacred because it comes from God, but it is usually practiced through human beings whom God calls to this ministry. But entering a hospital or hospice under the prospect of terminal illness calls us to a more profound ministry. The ministry is still healing, but healing on a different dimension. The hospice patient and his or her family and friends enter as a community, a community of suffering, but also a community of hope. This hope rests on the life, suffering, death, and resurrection of Jesus Christ. The terminal patient is called to radical discipleship. This involves renunciation of physical life and its opportunities and comforts, as well as renunciation of one's usual place in the family or in one's occupation or profession. In a very real sense it involves taking up one's cross and imitating, to some degree, the passion of Jesus. The hospice is the wayside inn on the highway to eternal life and our friends and caretakers are fellow travelers who will accompany us only so far. At a certain point we must bid them "Farewell" or "Au revoir" ("See you again"). Our ways part for a time and our hope is that one day we will meet again. Radical discipleship is arduous. The disciple will stumble time and again. There will be doubts, frustrations, and despair. But we travel toward our high priest who empathizes with our weakness, for he, also, was tempted like us (Hebrews 4:14-16). The apprehension of the terminal patient is well expressed in Christina Rossetti's poem, "Up Hill." The dying person asks an anxious question and his or her companion gives an honest reply:

Does the road wind up hill all the way?
Yes, to the very end.
Will the day's journey take the whole long day?
From morn to night, my friend.
But is there for the night a resting-place?
A roof for when the slow dark hours begin.
May not the darkness hide it from my face?
You cannot miss that inn.
Shall I meet other wayfarers at night?
Those who have gone before.
Then must I knock, or call when just in sight?
They will not keep you standing at that door.
Shall I find comfort, travel-sore and weary?
Of labour you shall find the sum.
Will there be beds for me and all who seek?
Yea, beds for all who come.

Our first reading comes from the book of Sirach, one of the Wisdom books of Scripture. It orientates us toward the healing ministry:

Honor the physician with the honor due him (her), according to your need of him (her), for the Lord created the physician; for healing comes from the Most High, and the physician will receive a gift from the king. The skill of the physician lifts up his (her) head, and in the presence of great people he (she) is admired. The Lord created medicines from the earth, and a sensible person will not despise them. Was not water made sweet with a tree in order that God's power might be known? And God gave skill to human beings that God might be glorified in these marvelous works. By them God heals and takes away pain; the pharmacist makes of them a compound.

(Sirach 38:1–8)

Patient's Prayer
God, our creator,
    you share with men and women
    the sacred ministry of healing.
Grant to my medical team
    the gift of discernment
    to diagnose correctly
and the gift of wisdom
    to heal me.
Give me patience, fortitude,
    and the elegance of graciousness.
We ask this through Jesus
    whose healing power has been poured on many
    throughout the ages. Amen.

Companion's Prayer
Holy Spirit, Good Counselor,
    be with us all in this moment of crisis.
Speak through us the words that we ourselves are unable to express
    so that we may strengthen and comfort
    our friend N. in all his (her) needs.
Teach us to communicate through word and silence,
    through touch and kindly gesture. Amen.

Prayer Together
Companion   May God come with healing in his (her) wings
Patient   And may I be ready to accept the healing that

God desires.

Companion	May God bless us with divine love and fortitude
Patient	And send us the Holy Spirit, the Comforter.

Prayer for Others

Patient	For those without medical resources,
Companion	Let us pray to God.
Patient	For those who are terminally ill,
Companion	Let us pray to God.
Patient	May the grace of Our Lord Jesus Christ, the love of God, and the fellowship of the Holy Spirit be with us all. Amen.

Reflections

John Keats (1795–1821) died slowly of tuberculosis. This is one of his reflections.

Darkling I listen; and for many a time
I have been half in love with easeful Death,
Call'd him soft names in many a mused rhyme,
To take into the air my quiet breath;
Now more than ever seems it rich to die,
To cease upon the midnight with no pain,
While thou art pouring forth thy soul abroad
In such ecstasy!
. . .

(John Keats, "Ode to a Nightingale")

6

The Invitation to Travel

But heaven hath a hand in these events,
To whose high will we bound our calm contents.

(Richard II 5, 2, 37)

There are few more traumatic moments in life than those in which a doctor tells a patient that she or he has a "terminal" disease and has only a short time to live. But the Christian can struggle with the question of whether this illness brings an end or a beginning. Is not the process of dying like the process of physical birth? There is pain, labor, and fear, but these lead to new life. In baptism we die with Christ in order to rise with him. In the physical process of dying, the seed of life is planted secretly like the seed of wheat, and the gestation period brings new life. Let us listen to the words of Paul, the apostle, when he was in prison and thought that death was imminent.

For to me to live is Christ, and to die is gain. If it is to be life in the flesh, that means fruitful labor for me. Yet which I shall choose I cannot tell. I am hard pressed between the two. My desire is to depart and be with Christ, for that is far better. But to remain in the flesh is more necessary on your account. Convinced of this, I know that I shall remain and continue with you all, for your progress and joy in the faith, so that in me you may have ample cause to glory in Christ Jesus, because of my coming to you again.

(Philippians 1:21–26)

Patient's Prayer
God, you have power over life and death.

You ask me to travel the highway of death.
I do not accept your summons
without anger and resentment.
You take from me that which is most precious to me.
Help me to weather the storm.
In fear let me find faith;
in pain let me find courage;
in horror let me find love, peace, and understanding.
Through Jesus, our brother,
who himself cringed before Death
in its vilest form. Amen.

Companion's Prayer
Jesus, you wept over your friend, Lazarus.
Weep with us now.
Give us strength for this journey.
Give us sensitivity to the needs and wishes of N.
May we be true companions
giving what is asked
and withholding what is not desired.
Hold us in your compassionate arms.
Let us feel your resurrected presence. Amen.

Prayer Together

Companion	For the courage to accept this diagnosis
Patient	And not hide behind denial, we pray to God.
Companion	For the grace to embrace understandable anger
Patient	And to direct our emotions rightly, and with justice and love, we pray to God.
Companion	For freedom of speech and wisdom to share our grief
Patient	So that our communications may be simple, loving, and trustful, we pray to God.
Companion	For the grace of communication with the risen Christ
Patient	And the presence of the Spirit who helps us in our weakness, we pray to God.

Companion	For all those who are affected by this impending death
Patient	That there may be a covenant of love and honesty between us, we pray to God.
Companion	All this we ask through Jesus, who experienced both pain and joy in his human life.
Patient	Hear our prayer, Jesus, our brother.

Prayer for Others

Companion	For those without medical resources,
Patient	We pray to God.
Companion	For those facing death alone,
Patient	We pray to God.
Companion	The grace of our Lord Jesus Christ be with us.
Patient	Amen.

Reflections

You bore, oh Virgin and Princess,
Jesus, whose Kingdom never ends—
Our Lord took on our littleness,
and walked the world to save his friends—
he gave his lovely youth to death,
that's why I say to my last breath
in this faith let me live and die.

(Francois Villon)

But true love is a durable fire,
In the mind ever burning,
Never sick, never old, never dead,
From itself never turning.

(Sir Walter Raleigh)

7

The Goal of the Journey

From this earth's thraldom to the joys of heaven.
(Richard III 1, 4, 255)

For the hospice patient the goal of the journey is union with God and eternal felicity. But we travel an unknown path to an unknown destination. We need, therefore, to carry with us the sacred vessel of hope and the flame of faith. As the author of the Letter to the Hebrews says: "Faith is confident assurance concerning what we hope for, and conviction about things we do not see" (Hebrews 11:1). When Jesus sat at table with his friends for the last time before his death, he explained the destiny of his own journey. Let us listen to his words.

Let not your hearts be troubled; believe in God, believe also in me. In my Father's house are many rooms; if it were not so, would I have told you that I go to prepare a place for you? And when I go and prepare a place for you, I will come again and will take you to myself, that where I am you may be also. And you know the way where I am going.
(John 14:1–4)

Patient's Prayer
God of Hope, my whole horizon looks bleak.
    Through the fog of confusion and hopelessness
teach us to seek the things that are not seen,
    those treasures in store for us.
Eye has not seen,
    ear has not heard,
    what you have prepared

for those who love you. Amen.

Companion's Prayer
>God of love and compassion,
>>give us hope and discernment.
>Through pain and suffering
>>may we lift our eyes to a new horizon.
>May the sun rising each morning
>>kindle within us
>the constant rebirth of hope and love. Amen.

Prayer Together

Patient	Eye has not seen and ear has not heard
Companion	What God has promised for those who love him.
Patient	For the gift of understanding and hope
Companion	In God's rich mercy and the communion of saints;
Patient	For the gift of peace and understanding
Companion	Toward God and our human friends;
Patient	For the joy of anticipation
Companion	And measureless faith;
Patient	For an appreciation of every detail of life
Companion	And the ability to enjoy moments of remission;
Patient	We pray to God.

Prayer for Others

Patient	For those who have no belief in the afterlife,
Companion	We pray to God.
Patient	For those persecuted for their faith,
Companion	We pray to God.
Patient	The Communion of the Holy Spirit be with us.
Companion	Amen.

Reflections
>The journey nears the road-end
>>where the shadows deepen with death.
>The setting sun unties the last strings of its gifts,
>>Squanders gold with both hands.
>Death is lighted with festive colors;

Life is before me.
With this word my breath will stop:
    I loved.
Love's overbrimming mystery
    joins death and life. It
Has filled my cup of pain
    with joy.
. . .

In the midst of agony and striving
    The door suddenly opened.
I gained the right of birth;
    That glory was mine.
I shared the stream that flows from ages,
    in wisdom, work, and thought.

If a vision were mine
    It belonged to all.
. . .

The quiet sky reached me,
    At dawn I received the radiance.
My death will be fulfilled
    In this earth with the splendor of life.

Today in the farewell of the year,
    Death, remove your veil.
Much has fallen aside, love's tenderness often left me,
    Lightless memory faded on the road
But at this deathless moment of life, O Death
    Your hands are filled with treasure.

                    (Rabindranath Tagore,
              "The Journey Nears the Road-End")

8

For Those Who Welcome Death

Never so truly happy, my good Cromwell.
I know myself now; and I feel within me
A peace above all earthly dignities,
A still and quiet conscience. The king has cured me,
I humbly thank his grace; and from these shoulders,
These ruin'd pillars, out of pity, taken
A load would sink a navy, too much honour:
O, 'tis burden, Cromwell, 'tis a burden,
Too heavy for a man that hopes for heaven!
                    (*Henry VIII* 3, 2, 385ff)

Although it is natural to fear death, there are many people who anticipate death with joy. This is especially true of those ripe in years. As Job expresses it: "You shall approach the grave in full vigor as a shock of grain comes in its season" (Job 5:26). But this may also be valid for those in extreme physical pain or in unnatural circumstances, such as in the case of hostages, prisoners, bereaved spouses, and many more. Let us hear the words of Paul when he was facing death in prison.

For I am already on the point of being sacrificed; the time of my departure has come. I have fought the good fight, I have finished the race, I have kept the faith. Henceforth there is laid up for me the crown of righteousness, which the Lord, the righteous judge, will award to me on that Day, and not only to me but also to all who have loved his appearing.
                    (*2 Timothy 4:6–8*)

Patient's Prayer
>God, beloved and ever faithful,
>>I rejoice that at last you call me to yourself.
>May my journey be in peace.
>>May I be surrounded by those who love me.
>May my body be without pain,
>>my mind alert, and
>>my heart full of joyful expectation.
>Comfort those who will be bereaved, especially N.
>>Bless my caretakers.
>Fill all of us with a lively sense of your resurrected presence.
>Amen.

Companion's Prayer
>Jesus, you bade farewell to your disciples
>>but you did not leave them orphans.
>You sent your Holy Spirit to them.
>>May the same Spirit help us
>>to release our friend with our blessing
>and may your Spirit work within us
>>the healing grace of grief. Amen.

Prayer Together

Patient	For all the joys and adventures of life,
Companion	Let us thank God.
Patient	For the grace to face death with serenity,
Companion	Let us thank God.
Patient	For family and friends, especially N. and N.,
Companion	Let us thank God.

Prayer For Others

Patient	For those who fear both life and death,
Companion	Let us pray to God.
Patient	For those indifferent to life's wonders,
Companion	Let us pray to God.
Patient	May the joy of the Holy Spirit shine within us. Amen.

Reflections

Come lovely and soothing death,
Undulate round the world, serenely arriving, arriving,
In the day, in the night, to all, to each,
Sooner or later delicate death.

Praised be the fathomless universe,
For life and joy, and for object and knowledge curious,
And for love, sweet love—but praise! praise!
For the sure-enwinding arms of cool-enfolding death.

Dark mother always gliding near with soft feet,
Have none chanted for thee a chant of fullest welcome?
Then I chant it for thee, I glorify thee above all,
I bring thee a song that when thou must indeed come,
come unfalteringly.
. . .
And the soul turning to thee, O vast and well-veiled
death,
And the body gratefully nestling close to thee.

Over the treetops I float thee a song.

Over the rising and sinking waves, over the myriad
fields and the prairies wide,
Over the dense-packed cities all and the teeming
wharves and ways,
I float this carol with joy, with joy to thee, O death.

(Walt Whitman, The Carol of Death)

9

The Itinerary

And death's dishonourable victory
We with stately presence glorify.
(*Henry VI* pt i, 1, 1, 20.)

One of the most moving and realistic descriptions of dying is found in Leo Tolstoy's short novel, *The Death of Ivan Ilych*. The author portrays vividly the physical, psychological, and spiritual sufferings of the patient and then his profound and sudden peace. One of his greatest burdens is the lack of honesty on the part of his family, friends, and doctors. They pretend that he is not dying when he himself knows full well that he is. At one point Tolstoy states: "This falsity around him and within him did more than anything else to poison his last days."

The dying person is called to face resolutely toward the heavenly Jerusalem, and yet many friends and relatives may reject the person because of his or her destination. The patient feels isolated and in strange surroundings: life is wholly disoriented. It is important that friends keep contact and try to deal honestly with the patient's situation. At the beginning of the journey it is sometimes good to speak openly with one's friends. This gives them "permission" to deal with the reality. It is hard to speak of death but much easier to speak of the eternal life toward which we are traveling. When the patriarch Isaac was nearing death he asked his family to prepare a meal, and afterward he blessed his son. The ancient Hebrews believed that this was an important blessing that released, as it were, a psychic soul into the community, a spirit handed down from parent to child, to grandchild, and on and on. Let us listen to the story of Isaac's blessing.

When Isaac was old and his eyes were dim so that he could not see, he called Esau his older son, and said to him, "My son"; and he answered, "Here I am." He said, "Behold, I am old; I do not know the day of my death. Now then, take your weapons, your quiver, and your bow, and go out to the field, and hunt game for me, and prepare for me savory food, such as I love, and bring it to me that I may eat; that I may bless you before I die."

. . .

Then his father Isaac said to him, "Come near and kiss me, my son." So he came near and kissed him; and he smelled the smell of his garments, and blessed him, and said,

"See, the smell of my son
    is as the smell of a field which the Lord has blessed!
May God give you of the dew of heaven,
    and plenty of grain and wine."
(Genesis 27:1–4, 26–28)

Patient's Prayer
God of the patriarchs and the matriarchs,
    grant me death with dignity.
May my mode of dying become a sacred memory
    to all my loved ones. Amen.

Companion's Prayer
God of the living and of the departed,
    grant us the grace to release our friend.
May his (her) spirit be kept alive in our hearts.
    May we be convinced that
his (her) life is changed, not taken away. Amen.

Prayer Together

Companion	Now I am going to tell you a mystery, we shall not die but be changed,
Patient	In an instant, in the twinkling of an eye,
Companion	The dead will be raised incorruptible.
Patient	Death is swallowed up in victory.

Companion	Thanks be to God, God has given us the victory through Christ.
Patient	My peace I give to you, not as the world gives but as Christ shared his peace with us.

[Patient may wish to impose hands on his (her) friends.]

Companion	May your peace rest upon us; may we share with you the fruits of the Spirit that God cultivated within you.
Patient	Let not your heart be troubled, believe in God, in Jesus;
Companion	May we have faith in God, hope in Christ, and love in the Spirit.
Patient	May the Lord make his (her) face to shine upon you and give you peace.

Reflections

My soul, there is a country
    Far beyond the stars,
Where stands a winged sentry
    All skillful in the wars:
There, above noise and danger,
    Sweet Peace sits crown'd with smiles,
And One born in a manger
    Commands the beauteous files.
He is thy gracious Friend,
    And—O my soul, awake!—
Did in pure love descend
    To die here for thy sake.
If thou canst get but thither,
    There grows the flower of Peace,

The Rose that cannot wither,
    Thy fortress, and thy ease.
Leave thy foolish rangers;
    For none can thee secure
But One who never changes—
    Thy God, thy life, thy cure.

                   (Henry Vaughan, "Peace")

10

The Clothing for the Journey

Give goodness its reward
Give journey safe through death
Give joy that has no end.
(Thirteenth-century hymn)

One of the most humiliating and depersonalizing aspects of hospital life is the constant stripping of the body for treatment, bed making, injections, and personal needs that a person in good health would normally cope with alone. Even wearing hospital gowns reminds one of a prisoner's garb. One is reminded of Psalm 22:18 quoted by John with reference to the crucifixion of Jesus: "They parted my garments among them, and for my clothing they cast lots." (John 19:23) As a person is stripped of material clothing, he or she can gradually try to don the clothing of the Holy Spirit. Listen to the words of the letter to the Colossians.

Put on then, as God's chosen ones, holy and beloved, compassion, kindness, lowliness, meekness, and patience, forbearing one another and, if one has a complaint against another, forgiving each other; as the Lord has forgiven you, so you also must forgive. And above all these put on love, which binds everything together in perfect harmony. And let the peace of Christ rule in your hearts, to which indeed you were called in the one body. And be thankful. Let the word of Christ dwell in you richly, as you teach and admonish one another in all wisdom, and as you sing psalms and hymns and spiritual songs with thankfulness in your hearts to God. And whatever you do, in word or deed, do

everything in the name of the Lord Jesus, giving thanks to
God the Father through him.

(Colossians 3:12–17; cf. also Ephesians 6:10–29)

Patient's Prayer
God, our parent,
    when we are stripped of our clothes
and others handle our bodies,
    we feel a loss of dignity.
Grant us poise and a sense of humor.
    Teach us to reflect upon your Son,
naked and jested upon the cross,
    —and upon all those who are degraded in detention camps.
Amen.

Companion's Prayer
Jesus,
    be with N. in her (his) humiliation.
Clothe her (him) with the Spirit of dignity
    and let the inner person grow stronger
as the outer one fails. Amen.

Prayer Together

Patient	Lord, make me an instrument of your peace;
Companion	Where there is hatred, let me show love;
Patient	Where there is injury, pardon;
Companion	Where there is doubt, faith;
Patient	Where there is despair, hope;
Companion	Where there is darkness, light;
Patient	And where there is sadness, joy.
Companion	O Divine Master, grant that I may not so much seek
Patient	To be consoled as to console;
Companion	To be understood as to understand;
Patient	To be loved as to love;
Companion	For it is in giving that we receive;
Patient	It is in pardoning that we are pardoned;
Companion	It is in dying that we are born to eternal life.

Patient   It is in dying that we are born to eternal life.

(St. Francis of Assisi)

Prayer for Others

Companion   For those who have lost a sense of their personal dignity,

Patient   Let us pray to God.

Companion   For survivors of the holocaust and Hiroshima,

Patient   Let us pray to God.

Companion   May we live in the freedom and dignity of God's children.

Patient   Amen.

Reflections

...Unborn, eternal, everlasting, this ancient one
Is not slain when the body is slain.

Who knows as indestructible and eternal
This unborn, imperishable one,
. . .
As leaving aside worn-out garments
A man takes on other, new ones,
So leaving aside worn-out bodies
To other, new ones goes the embodied (soul).
. . .
For to one that is born death is certain,
And birth is certain for one that has died;
Therefore, the thing being unavoidable,
Thou shouldst not mourn.

(The Bhagavad Gita)

11

Anticipatory Grief

Even through the hollow eyes of death I spy life peering.
(Richard II 2, 2, 70)

Although the patient may be the center of attention, we must not forget the caretakers, companions, and other patients. They begin the healing process of anticipatory grief before the death of their loved one. In a certain way this is beneficial because they commence their healing in company with the patient who can surely assist them. But watching their companion's grief can increase the patient's own pain. Like Jesus during his struggling journey to Calvary, the patient should be concerned about the welfare of his or her caretakers. We find Jesus doing precisely that in the following passage from the Gospel of Luke.

And as they led him away, they seized one Simon of Cyrene, who was coming in from the country, and laid on him the cross, to carry it behind Jesus. And there followed him a great multitude of the people, and of women who bewailed and lamented him. But Jesus turning to them said, "Daughters of Jerusalem, do not weep for me, but weep for yourselves and for your children."
(Luke 23:26–28)

Patient's Prayer
Compassionate Jesus,
   as Simon carried your cross, N. carries mine.
Be the sturdy strength of those who watch us suffer.

Give them the gift of tears to express their grief
and the discernment to see through the pain of the cross
to the healing dew of the resurrection. Amen.

Companion's Prayer

O God, your Son empathized with the women who wept over
him.
Do not forget those of us who suffer with N.
Help us with our cross
as Simon helped you with yours. Amen.

Prayer Together

Patient	N., may God bless you for your loving care, your patience, and your selflessness,
Companion	Hear our prayer, O God.
Patient	May God begin in you her (his) healing grace of anticipatory grief.
Companion	Hear our prayer, O God.

Prayer for Others

Patient	For those numbed by continual war and bloodshed,
Companion	Let us pray to God.
Patient	For the unborn dead who were not considered as human persons,
Companion	Let us pray to God.
Patient	May God's power be made perfect in our weakness; in all our frailties and mistakes may the strength of Christ tabernacle over us.
Companion	Amen.

Reflections

Now we face a paradox: on the one hand nothing in the
world is more precious than one single human person; on
the other hand nothing in the world is more squandered,
more exposed to all kinds of dangers, than the human being—and this condition must be. What is the meaning of

this paradox? It is perfectly clear. We have here a sign that man knows very well that death is not an end, but a beginning. He knows very well, in the secret depth of his own being, that he can run all risks, spend his life and scatter his possessions here below, because he is immortal. The chant of the Christian liturgy before the body of the deceased is significant: Life is changed, life is not taken away.

(Jacques Maritain, *Man's Destiny is Eternity*)

12

Loss of Authority and Power

I am not eager, bold
Or strong—all that is past.
I am ready *not* to do,
At last, at last!

(St. Peter Canisius)

Jesus' ministry began with scintillating success in the power of the Spirit. We see this especially in the Gospel of Mark. But his mission appears to have ended in failure and ignominy. He was reduced to the status of a criminal and slave. Let us listen to Paul, too, when he speaks about his own weakness and powerlessness.

But he said to me, "My grace is sufficient for you, for my power is made perfect in weakness." I will all the more gladly boast of my weaknesses, that the power of Christ may rest upon me. For the sake of Christ, then, I am content with weaknesses, insults, hardships, persecutions, and calamities; for when I am weak, then I am strong.

(2 Corinthians 12:9–10)

Patient's Prayer
O God, your Son emptied himself
 and took on the subservience of a slave.
Come to us who feel responsibility and authority
 slipping from our grasp.

Give us the authority of your Spirit.
   Temper our resentment and channel our anger rightly.
Teach us where true power resides—*in love*.
   Reveal to us the seminal power embedded in weakness.
Amen.

Companion's Prayer
   Jesus, our brother, look upon N.,
      who must relinquish her (his) former importance.
   Grant her (him) increased self-esteem.
      Enable us to help to call forth an even greater nobility
   and keep alive in our memories her (his) achievements and
      triumphs. Amen.

Prayer Together

Patient	He (She) who exalts himself (herself) will be humbled.
Companion	He (She) who humbles himself (herself) will be exalted.
Patient	The Son of Humanity came not to be served but to serve
Companion	And give his life as a ransom for many.

Prayer for Others

Companion	For those to whom no basic human rights are given,
Patient	Let us pray to God.
Companion	For those who take away the rights of others,
Patient	Let us pray to God.
Companion	May the God of peace, who brought up from the dead the great shepherd of the sheep, by the blood of the eternal covenant, Jesus our Lord, furnish you with all good, that you may do his will.
Patient	Amen.

Reflections
   The Soul's dark cottage, batter'd and decay'd
   Let in new light through chinks that time has made;

Stronger by weakness, wiser men become,
As they draw near to their eternal home:
Leaving the Old, both worlds at once they view,
That stand upon the threshold of the New.
                    (Edmund Waller, "Of the Last Verses in the Book")

Oh, that I were as in the months past!
as in the days when God watched over me.
While God kept a lamp shining above my head,
and by God's light I walked through darkness:
As I was in my flourishing days,
when God sheltered my tent;
When the Almighty was yet with me,
and my children were round about me...
When I went forth to the gate of the city
and set up my seat in the square—
When the young people saw me and withdrew,
while the elders rose up and stood;
The chief men refrained from speaking...
For me they listened and waited;
they were silent for my counsel...
They waited for me as for the rains.
When I smiled on them they were reassured,
mourners took comfort from my cheerful glance.
I rescued the poor who cried out for help,
the orphans, and the unassisted.

The blessing of those in extremity came upon me,
and the heart of the widow I made cheerful.
I wore my honesty like a garment:
justice was my robe and my turban.
I was eyes to the blind,
and feet to the lame was I:
I was father to the needy;
and the rights of the stranger I studied.

And I broke the jaws of the wicked man;
and from his teeth I forced the prey.
Then I said, "In my own nest I shall grow old;
I shall multiply years like the phoenix...
My glory is fresh within me,
and my bow is renewed in my hand!"

(Job 29:1–5, 7–9, 21, 23–25, 12–18, 20)

13

Loss of Freedom

Then death rock me asleep, abridge my doleful days!
(Henry IV pt ii, 2, 4, 211)

One of the more irksome burdens of any patient, but particularly the terminally ill, is loss of freedom. The patient is geographically, even locally, confined, often in the narrow space of a bed and at times with paralyzed limbs. There is little or no choice of work or recreation; there is little appetite and meals are tasteless. Only a select number of persons come to see the patient and often these are the medical team. One could make an endless list of restrictions. But above all there is no freedom of privacy. We might be reminded of Jesus' words to Peter:

Truly, truly, I say to you, when you were young, you girded yourself and walked where you would; but when you are old, you will stretch out your hands, and another will gird you and carry you where you do not wish to go.
(John 21:18)

(Or we might read the text of Philippians 1:12–14 or 2 Corinthians 5:1–5).

Patient's Prayer
O God, how terrible is the loss of freedom!
To feel like a hostage or jailbird!
Thank you for my former freedom,
    physical freedom,
    freedom to make decisions,

freedom to go where I pleased.
Keep me in mind of those unjustly deprived of their freedom
or under the abusive bondage of racism, sexism, or addiction.
Help me to work through my anger.
No one can shackle the Spirit.
Teach me of that new life
where time and space are no more. Amen.

Companion's Prayer
God, our savior,
you gave to man and woman
the unique gift of free will.
Look upon our brother (sister).
Light the lamp of hope
so that he (she) may perceive the new freedom
on the far horizon of everlasting life. Amen.

Prayer Together

Companion	That visitors may bring refreshment, interest, and, if possible, humor to this room;
Patient	That the world may come to me if I cannot come to it;
Companion	That the Holy Spirit may teach us a freedom that the world cannot give,
Patient	And that I might have the strength to embrace it.
Companion	We ask all this of God.

Prayer for Others

Patient	For those who abuse freedom,
Companion	Let us pray to God.
Patient	For those who are prisoners, hostages, or within detention camps,
Companion	Let us pray to God.
Patient	May the Lord bless us and keep us and let the divine face smile upon us and give us peace.
Companion	Amen.

Or

For we know that if the earthly tent we live in is destroyed, we have a building from God, a house not made with hands, eternal in the heavens. Here indeed we groan, and long to put on our heavenly dwelling, so that by putting it on we may not be found naked. For while we are still in this tent, we sigh with anxiety; not that we would be unclothed, but that we would be further clothed, so that what is mortal may be swallowed up by life. He who has prepared us for this very thing is God, who has given us the Spirit as a guarantee.

(2 Corinthians 5:1–5)

Patient's Prayer
Dear God,
    This earthly body decays.
Initiate us into the mystery of dying and rising.
    Give us faith that the illness of our body
will lead to our transformation in Christ. Amen.

Companion's Prayer
God of birth, death, and resurrection,
    as N.'s body grows weaker
may his (her) soul grow stronger.
    As you strip him (her) of physical facilities
Equip him (her) mightily with strength, wisdom, and beauty
of mind and soul. Amen.

Reflections
    Thy nature, immortality! who knows?
And yet who knows it not? It is but life
In stronger thread of brighter colour spun,
And spun for ever...
    But how great
To mingle interest, converse, amities,
With all the sons of reason, scatter'd wide
Thro' habitable space, wherever born,

Howev'er endow'd! To live free citizens
Of universal nature! To lay hold
By more than feeble faith on the Supreme!
To call heaven's rich unfathomable mines
(Mines, which support archangels in their state)
Our own! To rise in science, as in bliss,
Initiate in the secrets of the skies!
To read creation; read its mighty plan
In the bare bosom of the Deity!
The plan, and execution to collate!
To see, before each glance of piercing thought,
All cloud, all shadow, blown remote; and leave
No mystery—but that of love divine...

(Edward Young, *Night Thoughts*)

14

The World Shrinks

'Tis strange, that death should sing.
I am the cygnet to this pale faint swan,
Who chants a doleful hymn to his own death;
And, from the organ-pipe of frailty, sings
His soul and body to their lasting rest.

(King John 5, 7, 21)

In addition to the loss of freedom, the patient discovers that his or her world is shrinking. It is focused on the basic needs for survival, a monotonous, sometimes painful, routine of daily actions of washing, dressing, shaving, etc.—actions that were effortless and unplanned before the illness came. Listen to the words of Paul when he was confined to prison.

Not that I have already obtained this [resurrection] or am already perfect; but I press on to make it my own, because Christ Jesus has made me his own. Brothers and sisters, I do not consider that I have made it my own; but one thing I do, forgetting what lies behind and straining forward to what lies ahead, I press on toward the goal for the prize of the upward call of God in Christ Jesus. Let those of us who are mature be thus minded; and if in anything you are otherwise minded, God will reveal that also to you. Only let us hold true to what we have attained.

(Philippians 3:12–16)

Patient's Prayer
God, you created heaven and earth

and have given to human beings
the skill to travel to other planets.
My world has grown small, meager, boring, and ugly.
Help me to cherish your past blessings
and to look to new horizons. Amen.

Companion's Prayer
Help us, dear God, to bring the width of the world
into this one room.
Help us to soften N.'s isolation
and bring her (him) the warmth of friendship and concern.
Amen.

Prayer Together

Companion	That God may open up a glimpse of a new world to N.
Patient	And that I may begin to loosen my hold on this world.
Companion	That N.'s faith, hope, and love of God will enable N. to embrace this new mode of being,
Patient	And that my friends may give me freedom to take this step.
Companion	All this we ask of God.

Prayer for Others

Patient	For those who have never enjoyed a life of education, leisure, or comfort,
Companion	Let us pray to God.
Patient	For those poor in the world's resources,
Companion	Let us pray to God.
Patient	May Christ truly hold the planets in his right hand.

Reflections
And he said:
You would know the secret of death.
But how shall you find it unless you seek it in the heart of life?
The owl whose night-bound eyes are blind unto the day can-

not unveil the mystery of light.

If you would indeed behold the spirit of death, open your heart wide unto the body of light.

For life and death are one, even as the river and the sea are one.

In the depth of your hopes and desires lies your silent knowledge of the beyond;

And like seeds dreaming beneath the snow your heart dreams of spring.

Trust the dreams for in them is hidden the gate of eternity.

Your fear of death is but the trembling of the shepherd when he stands before the king whose hand is to be laid upon him in honor.

Is the shepherd not joyful beneath his trembling, that he shall wear the mark of the king?

Yet is he not more mindful of his trembling?

. . .

Only when you drink from the river of silence shall you indeed sing.

And when you have reached the mountain top, then you shall begin to climb.

And when the earth shall claim your limbs, then shall you truly dance.

(Kahlil Gibran, *The Prophet*)

15

The Circle of Friends Diminishes

And, father cardinal, I have heard you say,
That we shall see and know our friends in heaven:
If that be true, I shall see my boy again...

(King John 3, 4, 77)

The patient may also find that his or her circle of friends diminishes. People often stay away because they are afraid or embarrassed by illness and, more especially, by death. They may feel they may not know what to say to the dying person. Often, however, they stay away simply because the dying patient confronts them with their own mortality. Paul, the apostle, felt this lack of friends. In a work attributed to a disciple of his we read:

Do your best to come to me soon. For Demas, in love with this present world, has deserted me and gone to Thessalonica; Crescens has gone to Galatia, Titus to Dalmatia. Luke alone is with me. Get Mark and bring him with you; for he is very useful in serving me. Tychicus I have sent to Ephesus. When you come, bring the cloak that I left with Carpus at Troas, also the books, and above all the parchments.

(2 Timothy 4:9–13)

Patient's Prayer
O God, you have said that a friend is
    a sturdy support and the tonic of life.
Let me treasure the friends who remain with me
    and not resent those who have deserted me. Amen.

Companion's Prayer
> O God, Jesus said that he could not call us "servants" but "friends."
> Do not let N.'s friends stay away
>> through fear of death
>> or the unknown.
> Give us the grace to be as true to him (her)
>> as in the days when he (she) was well. Amen.

At this point some patients might like to reflect gratefully on the faithfulness of a spouse or a close friend. The following words of Scripture may help.

Praise of Spouse
> Children and the building of a city
>> establish a man's name,
> but a blameless wife is accounted
>> better than both.
> Wine and music gladden the heart,
>> but the love of wisdom is better than both.
> The flute and the harp make pleasant melody,
>> but a pleasant voice is better than both.
> The eye desires grace and beauty,
>> but the green shoots of grain more than both.
> A friend or a companion never meets one amiss,
>> but a wife with her husband is better than both.
> Brothers and help are for a time of trouble
>> but almsgiving rescues better than both.
> Gold and silver make the foot stand sure,
>> but good counsel is esteemed more than both.
> Riches and strength lift up the heart,
>> but the fear of the Lord is better than both.
> There is no loss in the fear of the Lord,
>> and with it there is no need to seek for help.
> The fear of the Lord is like a garden of blessing,
>> and covers a person better than any glory.
>>> *(Sirach 40:19–27)*

Patient's Prayer

God, our Father and our Mother,
   you said that it was not good for human beings to be alone.
Grant that my friends may come to me with few, but inspiring, words and gestures.
Let your Holy Spirit speak through them to me. Amen.

Companion's Prayer

O God, let your graciousness be on our lips.
   Let us speak the language of love and honesty to N.
to ease his (her) pain
   and strengthen our bonds of love. Amen.

Prayer Together

Patient	A kind mouth multiplies friends,
Companion	And gracious lips prompt friendly greetings.
Patient	A faithful friend is a sturdy shelter;
Companion	He (She) who finds one finds a treasure.

Prayer for Others

Patient	For those who have no friends,
Companion	Let us pray to God.
Patient	For those whose friends betray them,
Companion	Let us pray to God.
Patient	May God give us the gift of friendship to share with others.
Companion	Amen.

Reflections

Be careful, then, and be gentle about death.
For it is hard to die, it is difficult to go through
the door, even when it opens.
. . .
Be kind, Oh be kind to your dead
and give them a little encouragement
and help them to build their little ship of death.
For the soul has a long, long journey after death
to the sweet home of pure oblivion.

Each needs a little ship
and the proper store of meal for the longest journey.

Oh, from out of your heart
provide for your dead once more, equip them
like departing mariners lovingly.

(D.H. Lawrence, "All Souls' Day")

Because I could not stop for Death,
He kindly stopped for me;
The carriage held but just ourselves
And Immortality.
. . .
Since then 'tis centuries; but each
Feels shorter than the day
I first surmised the horses' heads
Were toward eternity.

(Emily Dickinson, "Because I could not stop for Death")

16

The New Life

Your wit makes wise things foolish; when we greet
With eyes best-seeing heaven's fiery eye,
By light we lose light; your capacity
Is of that nature, that to your huge store
Wise things seem foolish, and rich things but poor.

(*Love's Labour's Lost* 5, 2, 375)

The dying patient will oscillate between denial of his or her death, anger with human beings and with God, bargaining with God, withdrawal, and acceptance. The companions and caretakers may, indeed, pass through the same phases in their suffering and anticipatory grief, but, at any given moment, they will not necessarily be in the same stage as the patient is. This makes the choice of the appropriate words or dialogue particularly difficult.

I myself have been reluctant to introduce the subject of death to patients and friends. I think the answer lies in not discussing death *per se*—unless it is to answer necessary questions about the process of dying—but rather to discuss the next world and eternal life.

The basis of the Christian's faith in the next world and the immortality of his or her own personhood is, of course, the event of the resurrection of Jesus Christ. The earliest extant witness to the resurrection appearances of Jesus is a list in Paul's first letter to the Corinthians (15:1–11). The apostle lists some appearances that are also recorded in the Gospels and some of which are independent witnesses. Among these appearances he tells us that five hundred brethren, some of whom are still alive and some of whom have died, saw Jesus all together. Paul does not mention the resurrection appearances to the women, which we know so well from the Gospels. Yet it is of great importance that he tells us that this material concerning the event of the resurrection did not originate with him but was handed down to him. Thus is it much earlier than 51 or 53 CE, which is the date assigned to 1 Corinthians.

After dealing with the resurrection of Jesus, Paul discusses the resurrection of Christians. It is well worth reflecting on this material. Paul tells us that everyone will rise, not as a resuscitated corpse, but as a transformed person.

I should like to relate two incidents from my own life with reference to discussing resurrection rather than death. The first occasion was during the illness of my mother who had suffered a stroke and could not speak, although her mind was alert. A patient died in the bed opposite to hers and the nurses, pretending that they wished to clean the ward, requested that my mother move to the shared sitting room.

Now, Mother hated being grouped together with elderly people and began to weep copiously. When we were ensconced in the sitting room, I explained to my mother that the nurses were not cleaning the ward but removing the body of the lady who died peacefully in a coma or deep sleep. I told my mother that I thought her turn would come very soon and that she should think with joy about the people with whom she would be united. I listed a few of them, beginning with her own mother. Then because my mother adored the works of Shakespeare I said: "And you will also meet Bill Shakespeare." Instantly my mother's tears turned to laughter and she seemed filled with joyful peace.

The other occasion was the terminal illness of a young friend who was very accepting of her death. A group of us administered Holy Communion to her and we took the opportunity to pause after the readings (Hebrews 12:18–24 and Matthew 25:31–40) to discuss our views of the afterlife and the people whom we hoped to see. It was a profoundly moving experience. I hope it helped our friend. It certainly helped me.

In view of this I am including here some readings about the afterlife in the hopes that they will bring hope and consolation to all who are facing death and also to their friends.

Reflections

> For you have not come to what may be touched, a blazing fire, and darkness, and gloom, and a tempest, and the sound of a trumpet, and a voice whose words made the hearers entreat that no further messages be spoken to them. For they could not endure the order that was given, "If even a beast touches the mountain, it shall be stoned." Indeed, so terrifying was the sight that Moses said, "I tremble with fear." But you have come to Mount Zion and to the city of the living God, the heavenly Jerusalem, and to innumerable angels in festal gathering, and to the assembly of the first-born who are enrolled in heaven, and to a judge who is God of all, and to the spirits of just men and women made perfect, and to Jesus, the mediator of a new covenant, and to the sprinkled blood that speaks more graciously than the blood of Abel.
>
> *(Hebrews 12:18–24)*

Now there was a man of the Pharisees, named Nicodemus, a ruler of the Jews. This man came to Jesus by night and said to him, "Rabbi, we know that you are a teacher come from God; for no one can do these signs that you do, unless God is with him." Jesus answered him, "Truly, truly, I say to you, one cannot see the kingdom of God without being born anew."

(John 3:1–3)

Therefore, since we are surrounded by so great a cloud of witnesses, let us also lay aside every weight, and sin which clings so closely, and let us run with perseverance the race that is set before us, looking to Jesus the pioneer and perfecter of our faith, who for the joy that was set before him endured the cross, despising the shame, and is seated at the right hand of the throne of God.

(Hebrews 12:1–2)

I tell you this, brothers and sisters: flesh and blood cannot inherit the kingdom of God, nor does the perishable inherit the imperishable. Lo! I tell you a mystery. We shall not all sleep, but we shall all be changed, in a moment, in the twinkling of an eye, at the last trumpet. For the trumpet will sound, and the dead will be raised imperishable, and we shall be changed. For this perishable nature must put on the imperishable, and this mortal nature must put on immortality. When the perishable puts on the imperishable, and the mortal puts on immortality, then shall come to pass the saying that is written:

"Death is swallowed up in victory.
O death, where is thy sting?"
The sting of death is sin, and the power of sin is the law.

(1 Corinthians 15:50–56)

17

The Resurrection of Christ

O Lord,
may the end of my life be the best of it;
  may my closing acts be my best acts,
  and may the best of my days be the day when I meet thee.
  (A Muslim prayer)

For I delivered to you as of first importance what I also received, that Christ died for our sins in accordance with the
Scriptures, that he was buried, that he was raised on the
third day in accordance with the Scriptures, and that he appeared to Cephas, then to the twelve. Then he appeared to
more than five hundred brothers and sisters at one time,
most of whom are still alive, though some have fallen
asleep. Then he appeared to James, then to all the apostles.
Last of all, as to one untimely born, he appeared also to me.
  (1 Corinthians 15:3–8)

Patient's Prayer
  Jesus, our brother,
you rose from the dead,
  not only to give us hope beyond the grave,
but to be present and mingle with us
  in the daily events of our lives.
Let us hear your living voice in the pages of Scripture;
  let our hearts burn within us
when your presence touches us in the eucharist,
  and keep not our eyes from recognizing you
in our brothers and sisters. Amen.

Companion's Prayer
> Risen Lord,
> be with us in a special way
> > as our friend stands on the threshold of a new life.
> Let us send him (her) forward in peace,
> > let us not cling to things old
> but look forward to the new. Amen.

Prayer Together

Patient	Now I am going to tell you a mystery,
Companion	All of us are to be changed.
Patient	The corruptible body must be clothed with incorruptibility,
Companion	This mortal body with immortality.

Prayer for Others

Companion	For those who mourn without hope,
Patient	Let us pray to God.
Companion	For those dying alone,
Patient	Let us pray to God.
Companion	May the Risen Christ give you faith, may the Holy Spirit give you hope, and may the Triune God embrace you in divine love.
Patient	Amen.

Reflections
> Heavenly Master, I wud like to wake to the
> same green places
> Where I be know'd for breakin' dogs and follerin'
> sheep.
> And if I may not walk in th'old ways and look on th'old faces
> I wud sooner sleep.
> > (Charlotte Mew, "Old Shepherd's Prayer")

> Dear, beauteous death! the Jewel of the Just,
> > Shining nowhere, but in the dark;
> What mysteries do lie beyond thy dust,

Could man outlook that mark!

He that hath found some fledg'd bird's nest, may know
    At first sight, if the bird be flown;
But what fair Well, or Grove he sings in now,
    That is to him unknown.

And yet, as Angels in some brighter dreams
    Call to the soul, when man doth sleep;
So some strange thoughts transcend our wonted themes,
    And into glory peep....
                    (Henry Vaughan)

18

Prayer in Denial

Lord, remember me, when you come into your kingdom.

(Luke 23:42)

It is perfectly natural to enter a state of shock and denial when receiving a terminal diagnosis. There is no reason why one should not pray for physical healing, but we must also remember that God is omniscient, all knowing, and may have wiser plans in store. I well remember the tragic death of two good friends who had worked hard for justice for black South Africans. They were killed in a car crash. Some of us, however, reflected that it would have been their destiny to be imprisoned and perhaps tortured for their cause. Mercifully, they died before that happened. Listen to God's answer to Job:

Have you entered into the springs of the sea,
    or walked in the recesses of the deep?
Have the gates of death been revealed to you,
    or have you seen the gates of deep darkness?
    Declare, if you know all this.
Where is the way to the dwelling of light,
    and where is the place of darkness
that you may take it to its territory
    and that you may discern the paths to its home?
You know, for you were born then,
    and the number of your days is great!

(Job 38:16–21)

Let us reflect, too, on Jesus' fear of death:

> And he said to them, "My soul is very sorrowful, even to death; remain here, and watch." And going a little farther, he fell on the ground and prayed that, if it were possible, the hour might pass from him. And he said, "Abba, Father, all things are possible to thee; remove this cup from me; yet not what I will, but what thou wilt."
>
> (Mark 14:34–36)

Patient's Prayer
Compassionate God,
  Jesus cringed before death
and offered to you loud cries and tears.
  If it is your will,
let this chalice pass from me
  and restore me to health. Amen.

Companion's Prayer
God of love,
  Jesus bade his disciples keep vigil with him.
  Give us the strength to remain alert
    to the needs of our friend, N.
  Bring us all the refreshings of your Spirit. Amen.

Prayer Together

Companion	Fear not; I, Jesus, am the First and the Last,
Patient	The one who lives.
Companion	I died, and, behold,
Patient	I am alive forever and ever.

Prayers for Others

Companion	For those who must die alone,
Patient	Let us pray to God.
Companion	For those who die in extreme pain,
Patient	Let us pray to God.
Companion	The grace of the Lord Jesus Christ, and the love of God,

and the fellowship of the Holy Spirit
be with us all.

Patient   Amen.

Reflections

The dying patient is not yet seen as a person and thus cannot be communicated with as such. He (she) is a symbol of what every human fears and what we each know, at least academically, that we too must someday face...Your fears enhance mine. Why are you afraid? I am the one who is dying!

I know you feel insecure, don't know what to say, don't know what to do. But please believe me, if you care, you can't go wrong...If only we could be honest, both admit our fears, touch one another. If you really care, would you lose so much of your valuable professionalism if you even cried with me? Just person to person? Then, it might not be so hard to die—in a hospital—with friends close by.

(Anon., *American Journal of Nursing*)

Death and the sun are not to be looked at steadily.

(La Rochefoucauld)

19

Prayer in Anger

Have I not hideous death within my view,
Retaining but a quantity of life
Which bleeds away, even as a form of wax
Resolveth from his figure 'gainst the fire?

(King John 5, 4, 22)

Anger is another emotion that is both most human and most understandable. The Hebrew Scriptures speak of God's anger and the New Testament shows us that Christ was angry at times. We need to use our anger properly. The book of Job begins with an expression of his anger:

Let the day perish wherein I was born,
    and the night which said,
    "A man-child is conceived."
Let that day be darkness!
    May God above not seek it,
    nor light shine upon it.
. . . .
Why did the knees receive me?
    Or why the breasts, that I should suck?

(Job 3: 3–4, 12)

Patient's Prayer
    God of understanding,
Scripture says, "If you are angry, let it be without sin
    and let not the sun go down on your wrath."
Teach me to direct my anger properly,

and not prolong it unnecessarily,
so that I may gain peace of heart. Amen.

Companion's Prayer
Holy Spirit of Truth,
enable us to sustain our friend N.
to help her (him) maintain integrity and honesty
and show her (him) a gentle spirit. Amen.

Prayer Together

Patient	Be angry and sin not.
Companion	Let not the sun set on your anger.
Patient	Give us hearts of understanding
Companion	And love that endures all things.

Prayer for Others

Patient	For those angry without cause,
Companion	Let us pray to God.
Patient	For those whose anger never abates,
Companion	Let us pray to God.
Patient	May the peace of God which passes all understanding dwell in our hearts.
Companion	Amen.

Reflections
Many cultures—and not only "primitive ones"—witness to people's belief in the life beyond. They express it symbolically using language and symbols from their own lives. Here is an Eskimo poem:

And when we die at last,
we really know very little about what happens then.
But people who dream
have often seen the dead appear to them
just as they were in life.
Therefore we believe that life does not end here on earth.

We have heard of three places where men go after death:

There is the Land of the Sky, a good place ·
where there is no sorrow or fear.
There have been wise men who went there
and came back to tell us about it:
They saw people playing ball, happy people
who did nothing but laugh and amuse themselves.
What we see from down here in the form of stars
are lighted windows of the villages of the dead
in the Land of the Sky.

Then there are other worlds of the dead underground:
Way down deep in a place just like here
except on earth you starve
and down there they live in plenty.
The caribou graze in great herds
and there are endless plains
with juicy berries that are nice to eat.

Down there too, everything
is happiness and fun for the dead.
                    (Eskimo Poem)

For if its own evil and depravity cannot kill the soul, it is
hardly likely that an evil designed for the destruction of a
different thing will destroy the soul or anything but its own
proper object. So, since the soul is not destroyed by any evil,
either its own or another's, clearly it must be a thing that ex-
ists for ever, and is consequently immortal.
                    (Plato, *The Republic*)

20

Bargaining with God

Then he said:
> "Oh, let not the Lord be angry,
> and I will speak again but this once.
> Suppose ten are found there."

He answered,
> "For the sake of ten
> I will not destroy it."

(Genesis 18:32)

Another stage that the terminal patient may experience is the wish to bargain with God. It might comfort him or her to know that both Jews and Christians—and perhaps most religions—find little wrong with this. Bargaining is one form of intercession. There are two famous "bargaining" texts in the Hebrew Scriptures. The first one is Abraham's bargaining with God to save the people of Sodom (Genesis 18:16-33). It is a long passage but well worth perusal. Below I give the second text, about good King Hezekiah:

In those days when Hezekiah was mortally ill, Isaiah the prophet the son of Amoz came to him, and said to him. "Thus says the Lord: Put your house in order; for you are about to die, you shall not recover." Then Hezekiah turned his face to the wall, and prayed to the Lord, and said, "O Lord, remember now, how faithfully and wholeheartedly I conducted myself in your presence, doing what was pleasing to you!" And Hezekiah wept bitterly. Then the word of the Lord came to Isaiah. "Go, tell Hezekiah: Thus says the Lord, the God of your father, David: I have heard your prayer and seen your tears, I will heal you: in three days you shall go up to the Lord's temple; I will add fifteen years to your life."

(Isaiah 38:1–5)

Patient's Prayer

God of Abraham and Sarah,
In the spirit of Abraham and of Hezekiah
I plead with you to prolong my life.
May it be a life of service and love
enriched and refined by this present suffering. Amen.

Companion's Prayer

God of healing,
you showed your compassionate love
through your Son's ministry of healing.
Touch N., our friend, now with your healing hands
so that we may rejoice in his (her) restoration to us. Amen.

Prayer Together

Companion   Once I said in the noontide of life I must depart.
Patient   You have folded up my life like a weaver who severs the last thread.
Companion   But you have preserved my life
Patient   The living, the living give you thanks, as I do to-day.

Prayer for Others

Patient   For those who long to die and death delays,
Companion   Let us pray to God.
Patient   For those who have come of age and would prefer to meet their Maker,
Companion   Let us pray to God.
Patient   May God's peace be in our hearts,
            to hope and yet to be accepting,
            to be accepting but yet to hope. Amen.

Reflections

> Death, be not proud, though some have called thee
> Mighty and dreadful, for thou art not so;
> For those whom thou think'st thou does overthrow
> Die not, poor Death, nor yet canst thou kill me.
> . . .
> One short sleep past, we wake eternally
> And death shall be no more; Death, thou shalt die.
>
> > (John Donne, "Death Be Not Proud")

> Lightless memory faded on the road
> But at his deathless moment of life, O Death
> Your hands are filled with treasure.
>
> > (Rabindranath Tagore,
> > "The Journey Nears the Road-End")

21

Prayer in Depression

Yet in this life
Lie hid more thousand deaths:
yet death we fear,
That makes these odds all even.
(Measure for Measure 3, 1, 40)

Depression is the constant companion of illness. Physical disability nearly always leaves us with a lack of energy, with physical, psychological, and spiritual weariness. Once again we can turn to Job and resonate with his feelings. But we should recall that in the time that the book of Job was composed there was no clear concept of the afterlife. Belief in the resurrection arises late in about the second century BCE and is proclaimed particularly by the Jewish martyrs, the Pharisees, and the Christians.

A Man that is born of a woman is of few days,
   and full of trouble.
He comes forth like a flower,
   and withers;
he flees like a shadow,
   and continues not.
And dost thou open thy eyes upon such a one
   and bring him into judgment with thee?
. . .
For there is hope for a tree,
   if it be cut down,
   that it will sprout again,
. . .

But the man dies, and is laid low;
    the man breathes his last, and where is he?
. . .

so the man lies down and rises not again;
    till the heavens are no more he will not awake,
or be roused out of his sleep.
                (Job 14:1–3, 7, 10, 12)

(Or read Acts 20:17–38, Paul's farewell to the people of Ephesus.)

Patient's Prayer
    God, you cannot be outdone in kindness.
        Look upon your friend in the depths of her (his)
depression.
        Send me refreshings from the Holy Spirit
and implant within me the seeds of hope and faith. Amen.

Companion's Prayer
    God of love,
        You came in the still small voice to Elijah,
when he was dejected and alone in the cave.
        Enable us to be that encouraging still small voice
to our friend, N. Amen.

Prayer Together (from Hosea 6)

Companion	In their affliction they shall look for me:
Patient	Come let us return to God,
Companion	For it is God who rent, but God will heal us: God has struck us, but will bind our wounds.
Patient	God will revive us after two days, and raise us up on the third, to live in his (her) presence.
Companion	Let us know, let us strive to know God;
Patient	As certain as the dawn is his (her) coming, and his (her) judgment shines forth as the light of day.
Companion	God will come to us like the rain,

like spring rain that waters the earth.

Patient   Amen. Amen.

Reflections
    Life is the desert, life the solitude;
    Death joins us to the great majority:
    'Tis to be born to Plato's and to Caesar;
    'Tis to be great for ever;
    'Tis pleasure, 'tis ambition, then, to die.
                        (Edward Young, *The Revenge*)

. . . When you see my hearse, say not "Parting, parting!" That time there
    will be for me union and encounter.
    When you commit me to the grave, say not "Farewell, farewell!"
    For the grave is a veil over the reunion of paradise.

    Having seen the going-down, look upon the coming-up; how should setting impair the sun and moon?
    To you it appears as setting, but it is rising; the tomb appears as a prison, but it is release for the soul.
    What seed ever went down into the earth which did not grow?
    Why do you doubt so regarding human seed?
    . . .
    When you have closed your mouth on this side, open it on that, for your shout of triumph will echo in the placeless air.
                        (Jalal al-Din Rumi)

22

Acceptance

Why so:—now have I done a good day's work—
You peers, continue this united league:
I every day expect an embassage
From my Redeemer to redeem me hence;
And more in peace my soul shall part to heaven,
since I have made my friends at peace on earth.

(*Richard III* 2, 1 5ff)

After many struggles the dying patient reaches the stage of acceptance but may go backward and forward even at this stage. She or he becomes more aloof from friends. This may prove painful to them but it is often a necessary step to the final release and the climax of the journey.

For we know that if the earthly tent we live in is destroyed, we have a building from God, a house not made with hands, eternal in the heavens. Here indeed we groan, and long to put on our heavenly dwelling, so that by putting it on we may not be found naked. For while we are still in this tent, we sign with anxiety; not that we would be unclothed, but that we would be further clothed, so that what is mortal may be swallowed up by life. He who has prepared us for this very thing is God, who has given us the Spirit as a guarantee. So we are always of good courage; we know that while we are at home in the body we are away from the Lord, for we walk by faith, not by sight. We are of good courage, and we would rather be away from the body and at home with the Lord. So whether we are at home or away, we make it our aim to please him. For we must all appear before the judgment seat of Christ, so that we may receive good or evil, according to what we have done in the body.

(2 Corinthians 5:1–10)

Patient's Prayer
> God, our Father and our Mother,
> into your hands I commend myself, body and soul.
> Grant that I may go forth from this life
> in dignity, serenity, and lively expectancy.
> Bless and comfort all whom I leave behind.
> May your Holy Spirit tabernacle over them. Amen.

Companion's Prayer
> Jesus, the hour has come,
> when you will glorify your friend, N.
> Give us the selfless grace not to impede his (her) journey.
> May he (she) go forth in peace.
> May your Spirit, the Comforter, dwell in our broken hearts.
> Amen.

Prayer Together

Patient	Wonderful, indeed, is the mystery of our faith.
Companion	Jesus was manifested in the flesh
Patient	And vindicated in the Spirit.
Patient	He was seen by angels, and preached among the Gentiles.
Companion	He is believed in throughout the world
Patient	And taken up into glory.
Companion	Wonderful, indeed, is the mystery of our faith.
Patient	May God bless us and keep us and lift up the light of his (her) countenance, and give us peace. Amen.

Reflections
Death must simply become the discreet but dignified exit of a peaceful person from a helpful society...

(Philippe Aries, *The Hour of Our Death*)

May I die at night
With the semblance of my senses
Like the full moon that fails.

(Robert Lowell)

O Lord, grant each his own, his death indeed,
the dying which out of that same life evolves
in which he once had meaning, love and need.

(Rainer Maria Rilke, *The Book of the Hour*)

I've noticed this: that no kind of death is so bitter but that it can be endured if one has resolved to die with steadfast mind.

(Desiderius Erasmus, *Colloquies*)

I am quite ready to admit that I ought to be grieved at death, if I were not persuaded in the first place that I am going to other gods who are wise and good
...and secondly...to human beings departed, better than those whom I leave behind; and therefore I do not grieve as I might have done, for I have good hope that there is yet something remaining for the dead, and as has been said of old, some far better thing for the good than for the evil.

(Plato, *Phaedo*)

Many have been willing to go to the world below animated by the hope of seeing there an earthly love...And will the one who is the true lover of wisdom,...not depart with joy? Surely he (she) will, my friend, if he (she) be a true philosopher. For he (she) will have a firm conviction that there, and there only, can one find wisdom in her purity.

(Plato, *Phaedo*)

There is a land of pure delight,
Where saints immortal reign;
Infinite day excludes the night,
And pleasures banish pain.
There everlasting spring abides,
And never-withering flowers:

Death, like a narrow sea, divides
This heavenly land from ours.

. . .

Timorous mortals start and shrink
To cross the narrow sea,
And linger shivering on the brink,
And fear to launch away.
O could we make our doubts remove,
These gloomy doubts that rise,
And see the Canaan that we love
With unbeclouded eyes,

Could we but climb where Moses stood,
And view the landscape o'er,
Not Jordan's stream, nor Death's cold flood,
Should fright us from the shore.

(Isaac Watts, "A Prospect of Heaven")

As the hind longs for running waters,
   so my soul longs for you, O God.
Athirst is my soul for God, the living God.
   When shall I go and behold the face of God?
My tears are my food day and night,
   as they say to me day after day,
"Where is your God?"
   Those time I recall,
now that I pour out my soul within me,
   when I went with the throng
and let them in procession to the house of God,
   amidst loud cries of joy and thanksgiving,
with the multitude keeping festival.
   Why are you so cast down, O my soul?
Why do you sigh within me?
   Hope in God! For I shall again be thanking him,
in the presence of my savior and my God...

(Psalm 42)

And now life in its turn has evolved death. For not nature

only but man's being has its seasons, its sequence of spring and autumn, summer and winter. If someone is tired and has gone to lie down, we do not pursue him with shouting and bawling. She whom I have lost has lain down to sleep for a while in the Great Inner Room. To break in upon her rest with the noise of lamentation would but show I knew nothing of nature's Sovereign Law. That is why I ceased to mourn.

(Chuang Tzu)

23

Occasional Prayers
On Making or Revealing a Will

Suggested Readings:
Genesis 48:1–2, 9–16
Psalm 20
Psalm 42
John 14:1–3

Patient's Blessing
May God our Father and our Mother,
   our brother, Jesus, and
   the Holy Spirit, parent of orphans,
bless you with threefold might.
   May they bless you in soul
   so that you lack no spiritual gift.
May you be blessed in mind,
   with Wisdom who sits by the throne of God,
   so that she direct your paths.
May you be blessed in body and
   the necessities of life
   and know that they come from God. Amen.

Scripture Prayer (adapted from Ephesians 3:14–19)
May Christ dwell in your hearts through faith;
   may you be rooted and grounded in love;
May you have the power to understand with all the saints
   what is the breadth and length and height and depth,
and to know the love of Christ

---

which surpasses knowledge,
that you may be filled with all the fullness of God. Amen.

Final Exhortation (Philippians 4:8)
Finally, brothers and sisters, whatever is true, whatever is honorable, whatever is just, whatever is pure, whatever is lovely, whatever is gracious, if there is any excellence, if there is anything worthy of praise, think about these things.

Final Prayer (adapted from John 17:24)
Gracious God, I desire that they also,
   whom you have given me, N. and N.,
may be with me where I am,
   to behold my glory that you have given me
in your love for me,
   before the foundation of the world. Amen.

Sleepless Nights
If in bed I say, "When shall I arise?"
   then the night drags on;
I am filled with restlessness until dawn.
   . . .
When I say, "My bed shall comfort me,
   my couch shall ease my complaint."
Then you affright me with dreams
   and with visions that terrify me.
                    (*Job 7:4, 13–14*)

Prayer
O God of peace,
   the psalm says, "So he gives his beloved sleep."
Yet I spend my nights as if I were in a raging sea.
   Give blessed sleep and peace of mind to me, O God.
Let my nights be an anticipation of that life
   where there is no weariness or tears or pain. Amen.

Reflections
I nevertheless remember that the feeling I experienced was

not very different from the satisfaction produced in men by the languor of sleep, during the time they are falling asleep.

(Leopardi,
Dialogue between Frederic Ruysch and his Mummies)

... my new vision of death; active, positive, like all the rest, exciting; and of great importance—as an experience. The one experience I shall never describe I said to Vita yesterday.   (Virginia Woolf, *Diary*)

For the gift of silence

Because both patient and caregivers are facing the unknown, they often resort to the kind of chatter and small talk that rises out of a sense of nervousness, fear, or a desire to please. But we don't communicate only with words. Nowadays we speak a great deal about "body language," the expression on a person's face, the wordless communication by gesture, the sigh, the smile. This form of communication is of utmost importance in the case of the terminally ill and their friends. We should pray particularly to be able to communicate without words. Silent prayer, the listening for God to speak, is often the best prayer. Music, also has a deep therapeutic and spiritual effect. I have included some meaningful refrains at the end of this book (page 131).

Listen to God's revelation to Elijah when he was depressed.

And Elijah said, "...I alone am left, and they seek to take my life." Then the Lord said, "Go outside and stand on the mountain before the Lord: the Lord will be passing by." ...the Lord was not in the wind ...the Lord was not in the earthquake...the Lord was not in the fire. After the fire there was a tiny whispering sound. When he heard this, Elijah hid his face in his cloak and went and stood at the entrance of the cave.

(1 Kings 19:10–13)

Prayer

God our Creator,
　　we wait in expectation.
Teach us the wisdom of brevity,
　　the power of gentleness,
　　　and the eloquence of silence. Amen.

PART THREE

Prayers in Mourning

24

The Bereaved

The bereaved person always finds that death comes suddenly even when the patient has suffered a long illness and when there has been abundant time to begin the process of anticipatory grief. The depth of grief and the length of the process of healing varies considerably. Many factors affect this, including the identity both of the deceased and of the bereaved—for example, a spouse, parent, child, born or unborn, and friend or acquaintance. The milieu of death is also of significance, whether the death occurred after a long illness or suddenly, tragically, violently, or peacefully.

Grief is normal and natural. Indeed, lack of signs of grief may lead to physical and psychological complications. The signs of grief can be seen in many types of behavior. The grieving person, for example, may disbelieve and deny the death, a denial that may lead to searching for the deceased, and to dreams or nightmares. The bereaved might experience social withdrawal, confusion, hyperactivity, or the lack of activity that C. S. Lewis called "the laziness of grief." In most cases there is a feeling of utter helplessness. Ordinary every-day things and occurrences may set off grief reactions—the chair the deceased used, the objects he or she treasured, doing work that the deceased was accustomed to performing, watching his or her favorite television program. More especially, the bereaved may sense the presence of the beloved and even assume some of his or her characteristics.

The task of grief is to work through the phase of denial, anger, and helplessness to an acceptance and new beginning until the deceased is a "cherished memory" and the grieving person is enjoying a fruitful and peaceful life. In this section I have tried to help you in many of these phases. The readings and prayers are meant to be read slowly, meditatively. If one verse or line is fruitful just repeat that and do not think that you must finish the entire reading. Do not hesitate to cross out a verse that may not help you personally or might even offend you. Aim to walk with Jesus, the incarnate God, through denial, anger, guilt, and helplessness, to new life. You might like to reread some of the prayers and reflections that you and your loved one used together.

It often helps considerably to have a prayer partner or a support group to pray with you and to give mutual support.

In Jewish post-biblical theology the Holy Spirit, called the Shekinah (the immanence of God), is seen as Mother. She herself goes through the process of mourning over the tragedies that afflict her chosen people. For the Christian, too, the Holy Spirit is the Comforter, the Strengthener, the Advocate (Paraclete), the Teacher. It is, therefore, very important for you to open yourself to the presence and guidance of the Holy Spirit. Here is one of the most ancient, exquisite hymns to the Holy Spirit. Theologically it is superb.

Holy Spirit, font of light,
   focus of God's glory bright,
   shed on us a shining ray.

Father of the fatherless (Mother of the motherless),
   giver of gifts limitless,
   come and touch our hearts today.

Source of strength and sure relief,
   comforter in time of grief,
   enter in and be our guest.

On our journey grant us aid,
   freshening breeze and cooling shade,
   in our labor inward rest.

Enter each aspiring heart,
  occupy its inmost part
  with your dazzling purity.

All that gives to human worth,
  all that benefits the earth,
  you bring to maturity.

With your soft refreshing rains
  break our drought, remove our stains;
  bind up all our injuries.

Shake with rushing wind our will;
  melt with fire our icy chill;
  bring to light our perjuries.

As your promise we believe
  make us ready to receive
  gifts for your unbounded store.

Grant enabling energy,
  courage in adversity,
  joys that last for evermore.

(Veni Sancte Spiritus, attributed to
Archbishop Stephen Langton)

It would be an excellent idea to recite a verse or two of this hymn each day or even during the day.

Soon After the Death

It was the swift celerity of his death,
Which I did think with slower foot come on,
That brain'd my purpose. But peace be with him!
That life is better life, past fearing death,
Than that which lives to fear; make it your comfort,
So happy is your brother.

(Measure for Measure 5,1,199)

When Mary and Joseph went to present Jesus in the temple a man named Simeon declared that now he had seen the Messiah, and he could die in peace. You might like to join in his sentiments, thinking of your friend who perhaps accepted (or welcomed) death:

The Song of Simeon
Lord, now lettest thou thy servant depart in peace,
    according to thy word;
for mine eyes have seen thy salvation
    which thou hast prepared in the presence of all peoples,
a light for revelation to the Gentiles,
    and for glory to thy people Israel.
                                          (Luke 2:29–32)

Prayer
Jesus, the first born of the dead,
    you have called your friend, N. to yourself.
Blessed be your name.
    Now look upon your friend (*name yourself*)
and help me to work through the pain of my grief
    to wholesome healing and acceptance. Amen.

Eternal rest given unto N., O God, and let perpetual light shine upon him (her).

Reflection
They shall awake as Jacob did,
    and say as Jacob said,
"Surely the Lord is in this place,"
    and "This is no other but the house of God and the gate of heaven,"
    and into that gate they shall enter
    and in that house they shall dwell,
    where there shall be no cloud nor sun
no darkness or dazzling,
    but one equal light,
no noise nor silence,

but one equal music,
no fears nor hopes,
　　but one equal possession,
no foes nor friends,
　　but one equal communion,
no ends or beginnings,
　　but one equal eternity.
　　　　　　　　(John Donne, *Sermons*)

Seeking the Beloved
　...where this heaven of beauty
　Shall shine full upon them...
　　　　　　　　(*Henry VIII* 1, 4, 59)

When you cannot believe that your loved one is dead, when you find yourself searching for him or her, you might find the following readings helpful. In the first one, from the Song of Songs from the Hebrew Bible, the beloved seeks frantically for her loved one.

Upon my bed by night I sought him whom my soul loves;
　　I sought him, but found him not;
　　I called him, but he gave no answer.
"I will rise now and go about the city,
　　in the streets and in the squares;
I will seek him whom my soul loves."
　　I sought him, but found him not.
The watchmen found me,
　　as they went about in the city.
"Have you seen him whom my soul loves?"
　　Scarcely had I passed them,
　　when I found him whom my soul loves.
I held him, and would not let him go
　　until I had brought him into my mother's house,
　　and into the chamber of her that conceived me.
I adjure you, O daughters of Jerusalem,
　　by the gazelles or the hinds of the field,

that you stir not up nor awaken
   love until it please.
            (Song of Songs 3:1–5)

Prayer
   Jesus, you have said "Seek and you shall find."
     Be with me as I search
   for a new relationship with N.
     Gently wean me from the past
   and let me live the sacrament of the present moment. Amen.

The next reading describes Mary looking for Jesus after his death.

They said to her, "Woman, why are you weeping?" She said to them, "Because they have taken away my Lord, and I do not know where they have laid him." Saying this, she turned round and saw Jesus standing, but she did not know that it was Jesus. Jesus said to her, "Woman, why are you weeping? Whom do you seek?" Supposing him to be the gardener, she said to him, "Sir, if you have carried him away, tell me where you have laid him, and I will take him away." Jesus said to her, "Mary." She turned and said to him in Hebrew, "Rabboni!" (which means Teacher). Jesus said to her, "Do not hold me, for I have not yet ascended to the Father; but go to my brethren and say to them, I am ascending to my Father and your Father, to my God and your God." Mary Magdalene went and said to the disciples, "I have seen the Lord"; and she told them that he had said these things to her.
            (John 20:13–18)

Prayer
   Jesus, you rewarded Mary's seeking
     with the consolation of your risen presence.
   Give me the grace not to cling to my old relationship to N.,
     but to rejoice in his (her) transformed presence. Amen.

Eternal joy give unto N., O God, and let perpetual peace rest on him (her).

Reflections

The survivor takes the brunt of the pain of death.

(Arnold Toynbee, *Man's Concern with Death*)

...passionate grief does not link us with the dead but cuts us off from them...It is just at those moments when I feel least sorrow ...that H. rushes upon my mind in her full reality, her otherness ...as she is in her own right. This is good and tonic."

(C. S. Lewis, *A Grief Observed*)

Habits and interests of the deceased may be taken over indiscriminately...A hitherto rather dull wife whose witty husband had died surprised herself and all around her by her newly acquired gift of repartee. She tried to explain this by saying alternately, "I have to do it for him now."

(Lily Pincus, *Death and the Family*)

25

Mourning I

King Philip: You are as fond of grief as of your child.
Constance: Grief fills the room up of my absent child,
Lies in his bed, walks up and down with me,
Puts on his pretty looks, repeats his words,
Remembers me of all his gracious parts,
Stuffs out his vacant garments with his form;
Then, have I reason to be fond of grief.
Fare you well: had you such a loss as I could give
better comfort than you do.

(King John 3, 4)

The dead must be mourned, not so much for their own sake, but rather for the sake of the bereaved. As Toynbee says "The survivor takes the brunt of the pain of death." We should pray for the repose of their souls but also for the repose of our own as we go through the grieving process. But that repose does not usually come until we have expressed our anguish. Many of the psalms from the Hebrew Bible, especially the lamentation psalms, can help us in this respect. Some of the prophetic literature can also help us. For example, The Book of Lamentations is a song of national grief over the fall of Jerusalem. The church has long used the *De Profundis* (Out of the depths) to express sorrow or repentance.

Out of the depths I cry to you, O Lord:
    Lord, hear my voice!
Let your ears be attentive
    to the voice of my supplication.

If you, O Lord, mark iniquities,
    Lord, who can stand?
With you is forgiveness
    that you may be revered.

I trust in the Lord:
    my soul trusts in his word.
My soul waits for the Lord
    more than sentinels wait for the dawn.

More than sentinels wait for the dawn,
    let Israel wait for the Lord.
For with the Lord there is kindness
    and with him there is plenteous redemption;
And he will redeem Israel
    from all their iniquities.
                    (Psalm 129)

Prayer
    O God, you have brought me down to the pit.
        Let me not wallow in my grief,
    but build up new hope and confidence. Amen.

Reflections
    But O for the touch of a vanished hand,
        And the sound of a voice that is *still!*
                    (Alfred Tennyson)

The little mare munched and listened and breathed on his hands. Surrendering to his grief, Iona told her the whole story.
                    (Anton Chekhov, "Heartache")

Down, down, down into the darkness of the grave
Gently they go, the beautiful, the tender, the kind;
Quietly they go, the intelligent, the witty, the brave.
I know. But I do not approve. And I am not resigned.
          (Edna St. Vincent Millay, "Dirge Without Music")

II

Grief is like a long valley, a winding valley where any bend may reveal a totally new landscape.

(C.S. Lewis, *A Grief Observed*)

The manifestation of grief is a natural part of bereavement. A stoic and tearless stance is less natural. The church in its wisdom has a prayer for the gift of tears, for tears are often therapeutic and even physically beneficial.

But other emotions, such as anger and despair, are also normal. So are physical reactions, headaches, nausea, or even more distressing symptoms. No feeling of guilt must arise on account of these emotions. We need to be patient and gentle with ourselves for some months and to attend to our various needs and those of our families and friends.

One of the earliest and most potent hymns of grief is found in the Bible and is attributed to David. He lost his king and the king's son, his closest covenant friend, Jonathan, in the same battle. The traditional lament used among the Hebrew people was a loud and penetrating wailing, not just the slow trickle of tears. The recital of this lament is very therapeutic. Note that there is an element of denial in David's lament.

Thy glory, O Israel, is slain upon thy high places!
How are the mighty fallen!
Tell it not in Gath,
publish it not in the streets of
Ashkelon;
lest the daughters of the Philistines rejoice,
lest the daughters of the uncircumcised exult.
Ye mountains of Gilboa,
Let there be no dew or rain upon you,
nor upsurging of the deep!
For there the shield of the mighty
was defiled,
the shield of Saul, not anointed

with oil.
From the blood of the slain,
    from the fat of the mighty,
the bow of Jonathan turned not back,
    and the sword of Saul returned not empty.

Saul and Jonathan, beloved and lovely!
    In life and in death they were not divided;
they were swifter than eagles,
    they were stronger than lions.

Ye daughters of Israel, weep over Saul,
    who clothed you daintily in scarlet,
    who put ornaments of gold upon
    your apparel.

How are the mighty fallen
    in the midst of the battle!

Jonathan lies slain upon thy high
    places.
I am distressed for you, my brother
    Jonathan;
very pleasant have you been to me;
    your love to me was wonderful,
    passing the love of women.

How are the mighty fallen,
    and the weapons of war perished!
                    (2 Samuel 1:19–27)

Prayer
    Compassionate God,
        N. was beloved and cherished by me,
    unlock the floodgates of my tears
        that I may pour out my lamentation to you.
    For you are God of Infinite Compassion. Amen.

Reflections

...for all pairs of lovers without exception, bereavement is a universal and integral part of our experience of love. It follows marriage as normally as marriage follows courtship or as autumn follows summer. It is not a truncation of the process but one of its phases; not the interruption of the dance but the next figure. We are "taken out of ourselves" by the loved one while she is here. Then comes the tragic figure of the dance in which we must learn to be still taken out of ourselves though the bodily presence is withdrawn, to love the very Her, and not fall back to loving our past, or our memory, or our sorrow, or our relief from sorrow, or our own love.

(C. S. Lewis, *A Grief Observed*)

26

Anger

Blanch: The lady Constance speaks not from her faith,
                But from her need.
Constance: O, if thou grant my needs,
                Which only lives but by the death of faith,
                That need must needs infer this principle,
                That faith would live again by death of need;
                O, then, tread down my need, and faith mounts
                up;
                Keep my need up, and faith is trodden down.

(King John 3, 1, 212)

Anger is also a normal response to death. This may be anger against God for allowing the person to die, or anger against the deceased or, indeed, against the one who has killed the loved one either through design or carelessness. The psalms are very helpful in expressing our anger. We must always remember that God is perfect in understanding and God is able to accept our anger if it is expressed in the right way. Try to express your anger in the words of the psalmist:

O Lord, my God, I call for help by day;
    I cry out in the night before thee.
Let my prayer come before thee,
    incline thy ear to my cry!

For my soul is full of troubles,
    and my life draws near to Sheol.
I am reckoned among those who go

down to the Pit;
I am one who has no strength,
    like one forsaken among the dead,
    like the slain that lie in the grave,
like those whom thou dost remember no more,
    for they are cut off from thy hand.
Thou has put me in the depths of the Pit,
    in the regions dark and deep.
Thy wrath lies heavy upon me,
    and thou dost overwhelm me with
    all thy waves.
Thou hast caused my companions to shun me;
    thou hast made me a thing of horror to them.
I am shut in so that I cannot escape;
    my eye grows dim through sorrow.

                            (Psalm 88:1–9a)

Prayer
    O God of patience and kindness,
        help me to give vent to cleansing anger.
    In its place give me hope and gradual acceptance of my loss.
        Amen.

Prayer
    O God, you came to Elijah,
        when he was alone on the mountain and yearning for death.
    Come now to me in that still small voice
        and speak to my heart. Amen.

Reflections
    To break in upon her rest with the noise of lamentation would
    but show that I knew nothing of nature's Sovereign Law.

                              (Chuang Tzu)

    Weep if you must, but sing as well.
                       (Joyce Grenfell)

Mine eyes sought him everywhere, but he was not granted

Mine eyes sought him everywhere, but he was not granted them; and I hated all places, for that they had not him; nor could they now tell me, "he is coming," as when he was alive and absent.

(Augustine, *Confessions*)

I dreamt of you again last night. And when I woke up it was as if you had died afresh. Every day I find it harder to bear.

...For this little room was the gleanings of our life together. All our happiness was over this fire and with these books....It is impossible to think that I shall never sit with you again and hear your laugh. That every day for the rest of my life you will be away.

(Carrington, *Diaries*)

27

Empathetic Understanding

... it was the death of the most virtuous gentlewoman that ever nature had praise for creating: if she had partaken of my flesh, and cost me the dearest groans of a mother, I could not have owed her a more rooted love.

(All's Well That Ends Well 4, 5, 9)

God, especially in Jesus, who is fully divine and fully human, can give us empathetic understanding. This understanding comes either directly from God *per se* or through the ministry of others. The spiritual gifts of the utterance of wisdom and knowledge are listed among other ministries by Paul in 1 Corinthians 12:1–10. Other important ministries are listed in Romans 12:7–8. You might like to meditate on these. Once again, however, we can now turn to the Letter to the Hebrews to discover why Jesus can be so full of understanding and compassion.

Since then we have a great high priest who has passed through the heavens, Jesus, the Son of God, let us hold fast our confession. For we have not a high priest who is unable to sympathize with our weaknesses, but one who in every respect has been tempted as we are, yet without sinning. Let us then with confidence draw near to the throne of grace, that we may receive mercy and find grace to help in time of need.

(Hebrews 4:14–16)

When the risen Jesus walked with the two disciples along the road to Emmaus, he explained to them the necessity of the suffering that precedes perfect happiness.

And he said to them, "O foolish ones, and slow of heart to believe all that the prophets have spoken! Was it not necessary that the Christ should suffer these things and enter into his glory?" And beginning with Moses and all the prophets, he interpreted to them in all the scriptures the things concerning himself.

(Luke 24:25–28)

We find the risen Jesus especially in the eucharist: these same disciples on the way to Emmaus recognized him in the breaking of bread (Luke 24:30–31). It is in the eucharist that we also communicate with the triumphant body of Christ, which is the communion of saints. Our friend is now joined to that community.

Prayer
> Jesus, compassionate fellow sufferer,
>> walk with us on the night of sorrow
>> and guide us to the dawn of a new life. Amen.

Dr. Patrick del Zoppo has devised a kind of acronym to express the goals of the bereaved. They should try to aim for:

H	honesty
O	optimism
P	persistent
E	Effort

While it is important to be quite honest with our feelings we must also gradually open ourselves up to optimism, acceptance, a feeling of security, growth, spiritual consolation, and confidentiality.

Prayer
 God of abundant hope,
  give us honesty to confront our situation;
  optimism to trust in your grace and our own;
  discernment to assess it;
  courage to embrace it,
  persistence in moulding it anew
  and joyful love to find a
  deeper peace. Amen.

Or

Therefore, since we are justified by faith, we have peace with God through our Lord Jesus Christ. Through him we have obtained access to this grace in which we stand, and we rejoice in our hope of sharing the glory of God. More than that, we rejoice in our sufferings, knowing that suffering produces endurance, and endurance produces character, and character produces hope, and hope does not disappoint us, because God's love has been poured into our hearts through the Holy Spirit who has been given to us.

(Romans 5:1–5)

Prayer
 Jesus, we know that suffering is
  the crucible wherein the fruits of the Spirit are refined.
 Let our sorrow be the fertile ground in which
  the fruits of the Spirit are cultivated. Amen.

Reflections
 When he went to the cafe that evening—
 he happened to have some vital business there—
 to that same cafe where they used to go together,
 it was a knife in his heart.

(C.P. Gavafy)

Every extraordinary person has a particular mission which he (she) or he is called upon to fulfill. When he (she) accomplished it, he (she) is no longer needed on earth in the same form, and Providence uses him (her) for something else...Mozart died at thirty-six. Raphael at practically the same age...But each of them had accomplished his mission perfectly, and it was time for them to go so that others might still have something left to do in the world created to last a long while.

(J.W. von Goethe,
Conversations with Eckermann)

28

Saying Goodbye

... let us here embrace:
Farewell until we meet again in heaven.
(Richard III 3, 3, 23)

When we have worked through some of our emotions we try to say "Goodbye" or "Farewell" to our loved one. There is an important passage in Scripture that may help us to understand this need. Listen to John's Gospel describing the acute grief of Mary Magdalene, a disciple of Jesus. She heard someone ask her why she was weeping. She supposed that the person speaking to her was the gardener, but discovered that it was Jesus himself.

> Jesus said to her, "Mary!" She turned to him and said "Rabboni!" (meaning "Teacher"). Jesus then said: "Do not cling to me, for I have not yet ascended to the Father. Rather, go to my brothers and sisters and tell them, I am ascending to my Parent and your Parent, to my God and your God!"
> (John 20:16–18)

Jesus' request that Mary should not cling to him is open to a number of interpretations. For our purposes, however, we can understand it to mean that Mary was not to cling to her old relationship with Jesus but rather to build up a new relationship to him in his transformed person. This is what we have been asked to do with regard to our relationship to our loved one who has died. We need to pray for faith in the afterlife. We can, of course, pray to the deceased.

Prayer
   Jesus,
   you took away from your disciples your bodily presence
      to be with them in even greater reality.
   Give us a lively faith in your resurrected presence
      and joyful hope that our loved one
   lives with you and among us in perfect happiness. Amen.

Reflections
   Oh, may I join the choir invisible
   Of those immortal dead who live again
   In minds made better by their presence: live
   In pulses stirred to generosity,
   In deeds of daring rectitude, in scorn
   For miserable aims that end with self,
   In thought sublime that pierce the night like stars,
   And with their mild persistence urge man's search
   To vaster issues.
   So to live is heaven:
   To make undying music in the world,
   Breathing as beauteous order that controls
   With growing sway the growing life of man.
   . . .
   Divinely human, raising worship so
   To higher reverence more mixed with love—
   That better self shall live till human Time
   shall fold its eyelids, and the human sky
   Be gathered like a scroll within the tomb
   Unread for ever.
   This is life to come,
   Which martyred men have made more glorious
   For us who strive to follow. May I reach
   That purest heaven, be to other souls
   The cup of strength in some great agony,
   Enkindle generous ardour, feed pure love,
   Beget the smiles that have no cruelty—
   Be the sweet presence of a good diffused,
   And in diffusion ever more intense.

So shall I join the choir invisible
Whose music is the gladness of the world.

(George Eliot)

I was not aware of the moment when I first crossed the threshold of this life.

What was the power that made me open out into this vast mystery like a bud in the forest at midnight!

When in the morning I looked upon the light I felt in a moment that I was no stranger in this world, that the inscrutable without name and form had taken me in its arms in the form of my own mother.

Even so, in death the same unknown will appear as ever known to me. And because I love this life, I know I shall love death as well.

The child cries out when from the right breast the mother takes it away, in the very next moment to find in the left one its consolation.

(Rabindranath Tagore, Gitanjali)

...the Paraclete, the Holy Spirit whom the Father will send in my name, will instruct you in everything, and remind you of all that I told you.

"Peace" is my farewell to you, my peace is my gift to you; I do not give it to you as the world gives peace. Do not be distressed or fearful. You have heard me say, "I go away for a while, and come back to you." If you truly loved me you would rejoice to have me go to the Father...

(John 14:26–28)

At the round earth's imagin'd corners, blow
Your trumpets, Angels, and arise, arise
From death, you numberless infinities
Of souls, and to your scatter'd bodies go,
All whom the flood did, and fire shall o'erthrown,
All whom war, dearth, age, agues, tyrannies,
Despair, law, chance, hath slain, and you whose eyes
Shall behold God, and never taste death's woe.

(John Donne, Holy Sonnets)

APPENDIX

Biblical Farewell Addresses

Acts 20:17–38 (Paul)

Luke 22:14–38 (Jesus)

1 Maccabees 2:49–70 (Mattahias)

1 Kings 2:1–10 (David)

Deuteronomy 31–34 (Moses)

Joshua 23–24 (Joshua)

1 Samuel 12:1–25 (Samuel)

1 Chronicles 28–29 (David)

Tobit 14:3–11 (Tobit)

John 13–17 (Jesus)

Jesus, Remember Me

Ostinato Response

J. BERTHEIR

Mixed Voices

Je - sus, re - mem-ber me when you come in - to your King - dom.

Je - sus, re - mem-ber me when you come in - to your King - dom.

Equal Voices

Je - sus, re - mem-ber me when you come in - to your King - dom.

Je - sus, re - mem-ber me when you come in - to your King - dom.

Accompaniment

Guitar
Arpeggiated

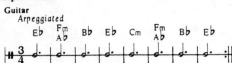

From the Collection *Music from TAIZE–Volume I.* Copyright 1982, 1983 and 1984. Les Presses de Taize (France). U.S.A. Agent, GIA Publications, Inc. 7404 S. Mason Avenue, Chicago, Illinois 60638. All rights reserved.

Eye Has Not Seen

Refrain based on 1st Cor. 2:9, 10

MARTY HAUGEN

Gentle and flowing ♩ = 96

REFRAIN

Eye has not seen, ear has not heard, what God has read-y___ for those who love him; spir-it of love, come give us the mind of Je-sus,___ teach us the wis-dom of God.___ (To Verses)

Last time to Coda

VERSES

1. When pain and sor - row weigh us down, be near to us oh___ Lord, for - give the weak - ness of our faith, and bear us up with - in your peace - ful word.
2. Our lives are but a sin - gle breath, we flow - er and we___ fade, yet all our days are in your hands, so we re - turn in love what love has made.
3. To those who see with eyes of faith, the Lord is ev - er near, re - flec - ted in the fa - ces, of all the poor and low - ly of the world.

(To Refrain)

133